Developing Highly Qualified Teachers

Developing Highly Qualified Teachers

A HANDBOOK FOR SCHOOL LEADERS

Allan A. Glatthorn

Brenda K. Jones

Ann Adams Bullock

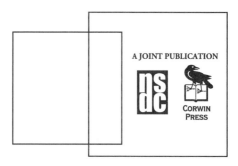

A JOINT PUBLICATION

CORWIN PRESS
A SAGE Publications Company
2455 Teller Road
Thousand Oaks, CA 91320-2218

For information:

Corwin Press
A Sage Publications Company
2455 Teller Road
Thousand Oaks, California 91320
www.corwinpress.com

Sage Publications Ltd.
1 Oliver's Yard
55 City Road
London EC1Y 1SP
United Kingdom

Sage Publications India Pvt. Ltd.
B-42, Panchsheel Enclave
Post Box 4109
New Delhi 110 017 India

Printed in the United States of America.

Library of Congress Cataloging-in-Publication Data

Glatthorn, Allan A., 1924–
Developing highly qualified teachers: A handbook for school
leaders / Allan A. Glatthorn, Brenda K. Jones, Ann Adams Bullock.
    p. cm.
Includes bibliographical references and index.
ISBN 0-7619-4637-3 (cloth) — ISBN 0-7619-4638-1 (pbk.)
    1. Teacher effectiveness—United States—Handbooks, manuals, etc.
2. Teachers—In-service training—United States—Handbooks, manuals, etc.
3. Effective teaching—United States—Handbooks, manuals, etc. 4. School administrators—United States—Handbooks, manuals, etc. I. Jones, Brenda K.
II. Adams Bullock, Ann. III. Title.
LB2832.2.G53 2006
370′.71′55—dc22   2005008041

This book is printed on acid-free paper.

05   06   07   08   09   10   9   8   7   6   5   4   3   2   1

Acquisitions Editor:	Robert D. Clouse
Editorial Assistant:	Jingle Vea
Production Editor:	Laureen Shea
Copy Editor:	Gillian Dickens
Typesetter:	C&M Digitals (P) Ltd.
Proofreader:	Theresa Kay
Indexer:	Michael Ferreira
Cover Designer:	Michael Dubowe
Graphic Designer:	Scott Van Atta

Contents

Preface

Everyone, it seems, understands the imperative need to develop highly qualified teachers. Yet relatively few seem to know what the concept means or how to achieve that goal. Even the federal government so far has been reluctant to provide answers to the schools.

This book is our attempt to provide research-based answers to these two urgent questions. As the table of contents indicates, the book is divided into four sections. The first section explains the foundations for the remaining chapters.

The first chapter answers the question, "Who are highly qualified teachers?" By reviewing the best research and by analyzing our experience as educators, we offer a clear answer. Since the issue is so important, we also offer several suggestions for involving the faculty in developing a sense of ownership about the concept. The next two chapters in this "Foundations" section provide several recommendations for recruiting and selecting highly qualified teachers.

The second section of the book explains two general strategies that involve all teachers. Chapter 4 will help you and your faculty develop your own differentiated system of supervision. Differentiated supervision recognizes the significant differences among teachers and explains how to capitalize on those differences in creating a highly qualified faculty. Glatthorn's differentiated model has been tested in numerous schools and has been found to be both effective and efficient. However, as Chapter 5 argues, all teachers need systematic and growth-enhancing staff development programs that foster their continued growth. The chapter also explains how to match staff development models to the strengths and needs of the school.

The third section presents six specific strategies for developing a highly qualified faculty. Two kinds of teachers get special attention: new teachers experience a quality induction program, one that helps them get off to a fast start in their careers. The other group needing special attention includes the few marginal teachers whom we have found in every faculty with whom we have worked.

Since most teachers are neither new nor marginal, the book devotes four chapters to the development of highly qualified teachers. Chapter 8 presents a rationale for using self-directed development for highly qualified teachers; Chapter 9 shows how to use teamwork in a "cooperative development" mode for quality teachers. Since mentors play a crucial role in developing highly qualified teachers, Chapter 10 explains how to make their work more effective. Although curriculum development is typically not seen as a method for developing faculty quality, Chapter 11 explains how it can be used in this manner.

The book concludes with two chapters that present the results of all this developmental work. Chapter 12 presents a comprehensive approach for retaining highly qualified teachers. The final chapter offers recommendations for developing faculty cohesiveness.

There are no simple answers to education's complex problems. However, if leaders can use these recommendations in developing highly qualified teachers, then school reform will become an achievable goal.

Acknowledgments

This book would not have seen the light of day without the significant assistance and guidance of several Corwin editors, especially that of Robb Clouse, who first saw the need for the work and provided guidance and support throughout the process. Others who helped in the production stages include the following: Jingle Vea, editorial assistant; Gillian Dickens, copy editor; and Laureen Shea, production editor.

We also acknowledge our indebtedness to the Pitt County (North Carolina) public schools for allowing us to use some material from their excellent guide for effective interviewing. Also, Jerry Jailall contributed a significant part of Chapter 4, using his excellent doctoral dissertation as the basis.

Corwin Press gratefully acknowledges the contributions of the following reviewers:

Dolores Gribouski
Principal
Columbus Park School
Worcester, MA

Carol A. Bartell
Dean
California State University
Los Angeles, CA

Joyce H. Burstein
Assistant Professor
Department of Elementary
    Education
California State University
Northridge, CA

Rosemarie I. Young
NAESP President
Principal
Watson Lane
    Elementary School
Louisville, KY

Phyllis Milne
Director of School Administration
York County Division
Yorktown, VA

Debbie Johnson
Principal
Lunt School
Falmouth, ME

Patti Kinney
Principal
Talent Middle School
Ashland, OR

Nora G. Friedman
Principal
Syosset Central School District
East Meadows, NY

Benjamin O. Canada
Associate Executive Director
District Services
Texas Association of
    School Boards
Austin, TX

Marguerite Pittman
Principal
Dutrow Elementary School
Newport News, VA

Denny R. Vincent
Principal
Muhlenberg North High School
Greenville, KY

About the Authors

 **Allan A. Glatthorn** is Distinguished Research Professor in Education (Emeritus) at East Carolina University. He is also Professor Emeritus at the University of Pennsylvania. He has been a high school teacher and principal, achieving a total of 55 years' experience as an educator. He is the author of more than 30 professional books, 6 of which have been published by Corwin Press.

 **Brenda K. Jones** is Associate Superintendent of Human Resources for the Pitt County (NC) School System. She has served as a personnel administrator for the past fourteen years. In addition, she has worked as a principal, assistant principal, teacher recruiter, mentor, personnel director, and classroom teacher in both public and private settings. She has published in the areas of mathematic instructional techniques, teacher recruitment and retention, and principal development. In addition, she has presented workshops on the following topics: teacher evaluation, new principal development, teacher performance appraisal, teacher dismissal, personnel employment procedures, assessing high-quality professionals, and teacher recruitment strategies.

 **Ann Adams Bullock** is Associate Professor of Education at East Carolina University. She is the coordinator of alternative licensure programs, preparing teachers for all levels. She has been especially effective in preparing teachers to teach at-risk students.

We dedicate this book to all teachers who see teacher quality as the overriding goal and the administrators and mentors who help them grow.

PART I

The Foundations

Understanding and Owning the Concept of Highly Qualified Teachers

There is much talk these days about highly qualified teachers. In fact, the No Child Left Behind (NCLB) Act of 2001 makes it clear that having highly qualified teachers is a keystone element of this federal design for reform. As of this writing, all new teachers hired with Title I funds must meet requirements of a "highly qualified teacher," and by the 2005–2006 school year, all teachers in the core academic subjects must be "highly qualified." However, the federal government has thus far been reluctant to specify what is meant by "highly qualified." This chapter therefore has two major objectives: to help you understand our concept of "highly qualified teaching" and to suggest a process by which you and the faculty can develop your own understanding of this key concept in operation.

UNDERSTANDING THE CONCEPT OF HIGHLY QUALIFIED TEACHERS

By reflecting on our own experience and reviewing the research, we have developed the conception of highly qualified teachers shown in Figure 1.1. As the figure indicates, highly qualified teachers have the necessary credentials: a bachelor's degree and full certification. Then they demonstrate competence in three major areas. Observe that the figure identifies three major components: quality learning, the science of teaching (which includes the essential skills and the subject skills), and teacher professionalism.

Figure 1.1 Quality Teaching

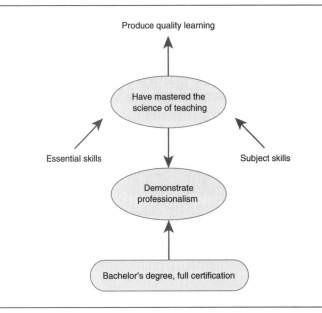

Quality Learning

As the diagram suggests, the ultimate goal is quality learning. All actions and measures focus on this element. This is the overriding goal: Highly qualified teachers get results, producing quality learning. Quality learning, as the term is used here, is characterized by the following features:

- It matters. It includes the core ideas of the disciplines. It leads to more learning.
- It is built upon a broad knowledge base. Both content and process are crucial.
- It involves problem solving. Students solve meaningful problems, using that broad knowledge base.
- It is learning that sticks. Students understand its importance and find ways to retain it.
- It requires active thinking. As students acquire quality learning, their minds are active, even though they may not be physically active. Teachers emphasize meta-cognition—thinking about thinking.
- It produces in the learner a sense of satisfaction and power. Learning is not always fun, but quality learning is often accompanied by a sense of excitement.
- It is best fostered by a teacher who knows how to give students the right degree of the structure they need to learn. The experts call that structure *scaffolding.*

- It happens best in learning-centered groups, as students share ideas, work together, and help each other learn.

While these general characteristics are usually in evidence, you will often note marked differences among students.

The Science of Teaching

What produces quality learning? The most important element is the science of teaching. The science of teaching includes the knowledge and skills that have been found by the research to produce student learning. In this book, the science of teaching is composed of two key elements: the essential skills and the subject skills.

The Essential Skills

The essential skills apply to all subjects and all grade levels. They have been strongly supported by good research and have stood the test of time. There have been several such lists. Those skills shown in Figure 1.2 have been synthesized from several major sources, including Cotton (1995),

Figure 1.2　Essential Skills of Teaching

Planning
1. Develops, uses, and shares problem-solving units based on curriculum standards
2. Provides and maintains a supportive learning environment
3. Uses group structures to maximize learning, keeping group assignments flexible
4. Communicates high expectations for self and students

Knowledge
5. Broadens and uses knowledge of community, subjects taught, students, and resources

Teaching and Learning Strategies
6. Communicates clearly the learning goals and objectives
7. Helps students discern, articulate, evaluate, and correct prior knowledge
8. Uses learning activities that extend knowledge, relate to goals, and actively involve students
9. Maximizes use of time for learning, using appropriate routines
10. Uses homework as additional learning opportunities

Assessment and Feedback
11. Assesses student learning, using classroom assessments as learning opportunities
12. Gives students timely and focused feedback on learning
13. Provides corrective learning activities for those not achieving initial objectives

Danielson (1996), Marzano (2003), the National Research Council (1999), and Rohrbeck, Ginsburg-Block, Fantuzzo, and Miller (2003).

The essential skills may be seen as the basics of effective teaching. Through numerous sound research studies, their use has been associated with improved school learning. As Figure 1.2 indicates, there are four planning skills. The effective teacher builds problem-solving units, drawing from the state's or district's curriculum standards and emphasizing long-term plans; the daily plans come from unit plans so that student learning is focused on the big ideas, not lesson fragments. And rather than focusing narrowly on student discipline, the effective teacher emphasizes a supportive learning environment that keeps students on task and engaged. At times, the teacher uses whole-class learning, at times small group activities, and at times individual activities. Throughout the lesson, the teacher communicates high expectations for self and students.

The teacher also has and draws from four areas of knowledge—the community, the subjects taught, the students, and resources for teaching and learning. Subject knowledge is perhaps the most essential. A teacher who has in-depth knowledge of the subject and knows how to make that knowledge of the subject accessible to the students is probably better able to help students master the subject.

Note that subject knowledge by itself is not sufficient. The teacher also needs "pedagogical content knowledge," the ability to make the subject understandable to the students (see Shulman, 1986).

The teacher also uses several basic strategies in fostering learning. The learning episode begins with a clear statement of objectives. Then the teacher helps students activate their previous knowledge, in the process testing and changing their concepts. The learning activities enable students to achieve the objectives, engaging them actively. Throughout the lesson, the teacher maximizes time for learning, using routines to systematize classroom processes. Finally, the teacher gives supportive and corrective feedback in a timely manner, helping the students demonstrate their learning.

However, these lists of the basics have been criticized on several grounds. First, the critics have questioned the soundness of the research that provides a justification for the skills. Such research, they note, has been poorly designed, showing a weak relationship with better learning. Also, most of those studies have been conducted in urban elementary schools. Finally, the critics note, those general skills ignore important research focusing on the subject skills.

Subject Skills

In response to that last criticism, many researchers have focused on the subject skills. These are skills that have been associated with increased

Figure 1.3 Subject Skills: Writing

The effective teacher of writing . . .
1. Builds a writing community in which students work together to improve communication
2. Emphasizes writing for real purposes and real audiences
3. Helps students use the writing processes flexibly and effectively
4. Helps students make appropriate choices about matters of form and style
5. Uses the technology to foster effective writing
6. Works with colleagues to emphasize writing as a way of learning in all subjects
7. Gives students constructive feedback about early drafts, helping students to revise

learning in specific subjects. For example, Figure 1.3 shows the Subject Skills for teaching writing.

If you examine carefully the writing skills, you will note that they provide a very useful supplement to the essential skills; they go beyond the basics. Thus, they are important in extending the basics.

You can use several sources in identifying such skills. The book *Best Practice* (Zemelman, Daniels, & Hyde, 1998) is an excellent summary of the subject skills for several subjects. The Macmillan publishing company has published several compilations, most having titles that begin with the words *Handbook of Research.* Thus, one compilation is titled the *Handbook of Research on Mathematics Teaching and Learning* (Grouws, 1992). Another similar collection is called the *Handbook of Research in Teaching the English Language Arts* (Flood, Lapp, Squire, & Jensen, 2003). You should also be able to locate sources on the Internet. Finally, most state departments of education will be able to assist you.

Teacher Professionalism

Finally, this conceptualization of quality teaching also includes teachers as professionals, who demonstrate week by week what it means to be professional, shown in Figure 1.1 as providing a foundation for the science of teaching. Some teachers view teaching as a job, doing the minimal responsibilities in a perfunctory manner and concerned primarily with working hours, salaries, and benefits. Some teachers see teaching as a vocation, a calling to serve in the classroom.

The professional sees teaching as neither a job nor a vocation. Instead, the professional knows that the impact of effective teaching goes beyond the classroom, affecting the families and the community. Figure 1.4 is one attempt to analyze the nature of teaching professionalism.

Figure 1.4   Hallmarks of Professionalism

1. Implements school board policies involving the classroom
2. Keeps accurate records of student achievement and uses data to increase student learning
3. Communicates effectively with students and parents
4. Has high ethical standards and acts ethically
5. Provides leadership in school improvement activities
6. Continues to grow professionally and uses constructive feedback for growth
7. Uses after-school activities as learning opportunities for students
8. Resolves faculty conflict constructively and cooperates with faculty in developing faculty cohesiveness

OWNING THE CONCEPT OF THE HIGHLY QUALIFIED TEACHER

While the previous section explained our concept of the highly qualified teacher, this section is concerned with developing in your faculty a sense of ownership of the concept. In this way, they feel that the results achieved represent them and their values. They will more strongly support a conceptualization in which they have had some input, rather than simply accepting a textbook definition. What matters most is for you and your colleagues to answer the question, "What is a highly qualified teacher?"

There are several ways to accomplish this task. Described below is a systematic process that has worked well in several faculty workshops.

Quality Learning

Begin with quality learning. Bring the entire faculty together for the initial workshop. At this workshop, have an expert update this book's delineation of quality learning. Provide time for faculty discussion in small groups. Invite representatives of the parent organization. On the basis of the update, the faculty discussion, this book's formulation, and parent suggestions, prepare a revised version of the nature of quality learning. Submit copies of this draft to the entire faculty, requesting revisions and suggestions. Use faculty input in preparing a final draft.

Focus Next on the Essential Skills

Use the same structure as above: expert update, small group discussion, faculty input, and preparation of final draft. Parents should be informed about the final draft; parent input is desirable but not necessary.

Move Next to the Subject Skills

Next, provide sufficient time and resources to enable team leaders or department chairs to develop brief summaries of the research in teaching a specific subject. Distribute the summaries prior to the faculty meeting. In the faculty meeting, give each group sufficient time to review the subject skills. Inform parents of the general results.

Now Focus on Teacher Professionalism

Invite a team of teachers to present a panel discussion of their concept of teacher professionalism. Invite a parent representative to offer a parent view. Develop a synthesis of these perspectives. Circulate the synthesis to the entire faculty, soliciting their input. Review faculty suggestions, making any revisions that seem strongly supported by teachers. Give each teacher a final copy of the synthesis.

USING GUIDELINES FOR LEADERSHIP

You can use any process you prefer in developing your own concept of the highly qualified teacher. In doing so, you may find the following guidelines helpful. They have been derived by analyzing our own experience.

1. Use an appropriate group structure. Rather than organizing one more committee, you would find it more efficient to use the groups already functioning. Thus, if you are the leader of a middle school where grade-level groups work together well, use a grade-level structure. On the other hand, if you are the leader of a high school where the department structure seems to work well, then you would be well advised to involve the departmental teams. The nature of the task forces will also influence group structure. For example, the essential skills should be determined by the entire faculty; the subject skills, by departments or teams.

2. Get multiple types of input. This is one area where diverse sources of input are desirable. Teacher input throughout the process is essential. Parent input is desirable when the issue concerns parents. How parents construe "highly qualified teachers" is critical since they are a key part of the educational process. Some schools have also invited older students to participate.

3. Take time. This process of developing faculty ownership of the concept of highly qualified teachers should not be rushed or treated lightly. You could do the whole job in one full day of high-pressure

work, but the result would probably not be high quality. While each faculty is different in terms of the pace of work and the demands of other tasks, most faculties who take the matter seriously spread the tasks over a term or an entire school year.

4. Deepen the knowledge base. You will get better results if those developing components of the vision draw from a deep knowledge base, rather than simply recapitulating their experience. That means that those leading the project should be sure that the work groups have available or can order books from this chapter's reference list and other bibliographies. How much reading they do will depend, of course, on the nature of their task and the total time available. Obviously, one essential piece of knowledge is further development by the U.S. Department of Education as well as state departments of education. Further analyses of what *highly qualified* means, then, should be integrated with your own.

5. See the process as ongoing. Both the process and the products should be revisited periodically to ensure that they are current and viable. Highly qualified faculty learn as they work together, and the products should reflect that learning.

A FINAL NOTE

Working through this process will take time and effort. However, principals who have used their own version of the process report that the discussions were an excellent learning experience for all.

Recruiting Highly Qualified Teachers

One of the first steps you can take is to develop and implement a successful recruiting program. This chapter suggests some effective strategies you can use in a comprehensive recruiting effort.

UNDERSTANDING THE NEED FOR RECRUITMENT

The answer to the question of "Why recruit?" is simple: There is and will continue to be a teacher shortage. So why is there a teacher shortage? That is a more complex question. Consider the following factors, as noted by Simmons (2000).

- More than one-quarter of all teachers are at least fifty years old. Retirement looms seductively.
- Many school systems may have smaller classes. Even though there is not complete agreement that smaller classes result in better learning, there is a strong and vocal consensus that smaller classes are better.
- Experts predict that by 2008, public and private schools will be expected to educate 54.3 million students, an increase of 6 percent over the totals in 1996.
- Many teachers leave the profession after teaching for only a few years. Some have been marking time until law or medical schools accept them. Some become disillusioned with the profession.

According to the National Commission on Teaching and America's Future (1996), working conditions and pay are driving qualified teachers out of schools where they are desperately needed. The report cited a lack of administrative support, insufficient time to collaborate with colleagues, inadequate resources, and discipline problems as contributing to teacher turnover and attrition. In addition, mentoring and administrative support, discussed in Chapters 10 and 12, are cited as contributing to retention of highly qualified teachers.

USING GENERAL STRATEGIES

Recruiting teachers so that you will have a large applicant pool is one of the most effective ways of improving teacher quality. This section of the chapter suggests some general recruiting strategies the school system can use to provide a sound basis for recruiting qualified applicants. The strategies can be implemented by the director of personnel or by a special recruiting team. A recruiting team is a group of select individuals who come together to plan a recruiting program. The following discussion assumes that a recruiting team will be chiefly responsible. (These strategies have been drawn chiefly from Clewell, Darke, Davis-George, Forcier, & Manes, 2000, and Simmons, 2000.)

Developing Partnerships

Developing partnerships can be an effective strategy in building the relationships that lead to more successful programs. Such partnerships should include the following entities: teacher training institutions, school systems, local government, teacher associations, and local communities. Such partnerships are successful only when genuine equality exists and meaningful openness prevails. All members need to be sensitive to the dangers of condescending and suggesting that they have all the answers. Partnerships with the business community can be especially helpful in offering positions to the spouses of successful applicants.

Preparing the Team

If you use a recruiting team, be sure that it is a diverse one. Typical representatives are the following: teachers, parents, teacher educators from universities, union members, district staff, school administrators, and community leaders. Also, be sure to train the recruiting team in developing the skills and knowledge it will need in recruiting teachers and being effective representatives of the school system. The following topics should be treated: area demographics, local features of interest to potential applicants, recruiting strategies, pitfalls to avoid, and school system policies and practices.

Gathering Information and Planning

The recruiting team should begin their work by doing some fact gathering. Here are some of the data needed: immediate and long-term personnel needs by school levels and subject specializations, activity sponsors and coaches needed, population trends, diversity of present staff, resources available, salary competitiveness, and turnover rate and reasons for leaving.

To understand the importance of the data gathering, consider this example.

Helen Foster, personnel director, is convinced that her school system must produce a slick multimedia production to attract new applicants. After she does some fact finding through new teacher surveys, she determines that the schools have a poor reputation because of poor test results, a lack of student motivation, and low school morale.

With the fact gathering completed, the recruiting team should make plans for its own work. One simple plan is shown in Figure 2.1.

USING STRATEGIES THAT RESPOND TO SYSTEM NEEDS

In addition to planning for recruiting, the team should undertake other recruiting activities that will respond to the special needs of the system.

1. Develop effective multimedia materials that present an accurate but positive picture of the school system, securing sufficient funds to develop quality materials. Be sure that they convey the image you wish to convey. Here are some effective strategies for making those materials more effective (paraphrased from Simmons, 2000).
   - Send recruiting materials to community organizations.
   - Use radio to reach older listeners.
   - Strengthen relationships with teacher training institutions.
   - Provide information about your school system to education majors at local colleges.

2. Authorize school-based teams to develop their own recruiting plans, so long as they are coordinated with the district's plans.

Figure 2.1   Recruiting Team's Plan

School year for which plan is made: 2005–2006

Personnel needed and authorized:

Schools	Subject Grade	Special Needs	Chief Recruiter	Recruiting Activities
Andrews Elementary	1 for Grade 2 1 for Grade 3	Reading Mathematics	Harris	Visit teacher education programs
Belmont Middle	2 Math/science	Sponsor girls' hockey	Ortiz	Register with middle school association
Carteret High	1 science Grade 9	Coach soccer	Rosenthal	Contact local scientists
Central office staff	Curriculum Coordinator	Computer skills required	Harris	Work with teachers association

Describe briefly plans for increasing diversity:

Contact Washington University to speak with sophomores on Career Day.

Washington University is a historically Black institution. Eight-five percent of the students are minority students; most have not considered teaching as a career.

Describe briefly recruiting activities noted above:

See attached page.

Date submitted: 2/24. Submitted by A. Henson.

3. Maintain close relationships with the chairs of the teacher education programs in nearby universities.

4. Recommend an incentive system to the superintendent. Recruiting teams have offered a wide range of incentives to teachers looking for employment: scholarships, forgivable loans, tuition waivers, summer employment, housing credits, transportation stipends, child care, and signing bonuses (Clewell et al., 2000).

5. Increase students' awareness of education as a career. Career day programs can use local teachers. Assist in the formation of Future Teachers of America clubs and other precollege programs. For example, South Carolina has instituted a Teacher Cadet Program, which focuses on very able high school juniors. As of 1998, the program had educated 20,000 cadets.

6. Form coalitions of the school system, community colleges, and universities. Such coalitions can promote recruiting by sponsoring such programs as "Why Teach?" days, coordinating curricula at all levels to ease the way for candidates.

7. Select "Teacher of the Year" for each level of schooling, from kindergarten to the last year of a bachelor's program.

8. Develop and implement a dissemination plan that uses local media outlets to inform the community about local needs and resources. Such dissemination activities should also include in the professional media articles about the program.

9. Develop a Web page that will provide information about the school system. One very effective Web page is that produced by the Clark County (Nevada) schools. Their Internet address is http://www.ccsd.net. You can use your school district's Web page to announce vacancies and search other sites to identify possible applicants. Here are some suggestions for making your Web page more appealing (paraphrased from Simmons, 2000).
   - Design your first page so that it looks like a magazine cover.
   - Begin small and grow as needed.
   - Update the site frequently.
   - Use lower case to increase readability.
   - Use focused graphics; too many graphics increase downloading time.
   - Make the site easy to read.

RECRUITING GRADUATES FROM ALTERNATIVE PROGRAMS

The general recruiting program described above provides a foundation for the efforts to recruit graduates of alternative programs. These alternative programs offer intensive programs for applicants who did not complete a traditional teacher education program. These alternative programs are designed to increase the pool of qualified candidates.

Are graduates of such alternative programs as effective in the classroom as graduates of standard programs? That issue has engendered much debate within the profession. The research is inconclusive. In a sense, the issue is not relevant for those recruiting applicants. The only immediate question is the qualifications and abilities of the applicants standing before you.

These alternative routes to certification have been developed by a large variety of organizations. Consider these examples.

State Programs

South Carolina has developed the Center for Teacher Recruitment, which provides leadership across the state in identifying, attracting, placing, and retaining qualified individuals.

Teacher Education Departments

Several higher education consortia and individual colleges have designed and implemented alternative programs, often in cooperation with state agencies. East Carolina University's teacher education office has provided leadership for North Carolina's schools in providing alternative tracks for hundreds of qualified individuals.

School Districts

The Houston (Texas) Independent School District has its own program to train interns in several areas of critical need. The program had trained more than 3,500 teachers as of the year 2000.

Foundations

The Wallace-Reader's Digest Fund has sponsored and funded the Pathways program.

Teachers Unions

The Chicago Teachers Union has provided leadership in the very effective Teach for Chicago project.

Individuals

As a senior-year project, Wendy Koop conceived, developed, and secured funding for the Teach for America program. Despite the success of that program, its future was in doubt at one time. Today, the organization has increased the number of training sites and has secured a major funding source. The program reports a solid foundation and is working on becoming an even more effective source of teachers.

EXPANDING THE SOURCES

School districts have also turned to several nontraditional sources for diversifying and expanding the applicant pool. Para-educators, who have experience in the classroom, are an expanding source of new teachers. They come with a general knowledge of your school and the community. Since some retirees find that retirement leaves them with too much time and too few meaningful tasks, they are likely to welcome the chance to teach. Retired teachers are an especially good source, especially if their health is sound.

Other sources have proved to be fruitful. Men and women who have been "downsized" in poor economic times will be eager to try a new profession. As with substitute teachers, teacher aides come with knowledge of school and community. Finally, military retirees have been well trained in skills that are transferable to educational settings and know the benefits of military discipline.

A FINAL NOTE

The teacher shortage is a state and national concern. Schools and school systems continue to search for ways to recruit highly qualified teachers. The success of a recruitment plan requires the cooperation of the entire school community. An effective recruiting program increases the applicant pool. In this sense, it is a key first step in assembling a highly qualified faculty.

Selecting Highly Qualified Teachers

Once you have recruited a good pool of qualified applicants, you then have to select the best. This chapter suggests how to select the best in three related stages.

STRATEGIES TO USE IN THE PRELIMINARY STAGE

Selecting highly qualified teachers can seem like an awesome task, both in terms of its importance and complexity. To reduce the complexity, we have structured the processes explained here in relation to three stages: preliminary, middle, and end. The processes can be used in any selection process.

This section focuses on the preliminary stage, recommending processes tested by research and experience. Of course, you should use your own approach if it has worked well for you in the past. Note that the process is very systematic and closely linked: a position is described; from the position description, the criteria are identified. Then the data sources are listed. The resulting matrix indicates for each criterion the sources to be used. The matrix is then used to develop specific forms.

In the preliminary stage, find answers to the following questions:

1. Who will be on the selection committee?

Three are recommended as essential: one school administrator, one teacher, and one member of central staff.

Depending on district personnel policies, you may wish to add a parent representative. And some high school selection committees have included a student. Be sure that the committee is fully informed about the research on both standard and alternative programs.

Note that the same individuals should all perform the evaluation tasks, to ensure reliability. All three should view the videotape the candidate has submitted.

2. What elements constitute the data sources?

For the sake of fairness and consistency, the personnel office should have delineated a standard selection process that would include the following data sources for all candidates:

- A completed application, including two professional references
- A professional portfolio that documents claims made about experience and training and provides evidence for the evaluation
- A videotape of the candidate teaching a class

The finalists should also be required to submit these work products: a unit plan based on state standards, an assessment of student learning, and a letter to a parent. The finalists, of course, will also be interviewed.

3. What is the position description?

Here be as specific as possible, but do not include trivial features. Figure 3.1 shows an example.

Figure 3.1 Position Description

> **Classroom teacher, primary grades.** Will probably be assigned to second grade. Must know current research in teaching reading and be able to apply that knowledge in planning and teaching. Also should know in depth the research on child development and its implications for individualizing learning. Should be able to use alternative means of assessment. All teachers are expected to have ability to communicate effectively in speaking and writing. Either qualify for state certification or alternative programs.

Special attention should be given to the important elements of the position description. It is designed to aid the selection committee; it is not a recruiting aid. It is brief and to the point. It focuses on the essential skills and knowledge. It does not include personal traits, such as hair color, size, or age. It does not include beliefs that candidates can pretend they have, such as this one: "We are looking for teachers who believe all students can learn."

The position description should enable you to specify the criteria—the qualities considered important. For example, consider this element from the position description.

Teacher should be able to apply the best research in the teaching of reading to his/her planning and teaching.

This results in the following criterion:

Applies reading research to planning and teaching.

4. What forms can be used to facilitate the selection process?

Several forms are needed to facilitate the process. Figure 3.2 is a very useful form—a matrix that lists all the criteria down the left and all the data sources across the top. The matrix can be used to plan the evaluation and also summarize the evaluation. Here is a simple way to develop the planning matrix. Consider each criterion. Which data sources are most likely to yield valid data for each? Put an x in the appropriate cell. Consider this a planning guide, with a copy for each assessor. When you have completed the first draft, review it with these questions in mind:

- Does each criterion have at least one data source?
- Given the resources available (chiefly time and personnel), is the plan feasible?

5. What evaluation code should be used?

Some schools use letter grades to rank the applicants: A, excellent; B, good to very good; C, satisfactory; and D, not satisfactory. Others use three numbers: 3, interview; 2, hold as standby; and 1, reject. All that matters is consistency.

6. What is the selection deadline?

Usually an early deadline is preferred. These preliminary strategies should ensure that you will develop a pool of qualified applicants, including several from alternative programs.

7. What aspects of employment law should the committee know?

To avoid serious errors in the selection process, all those involved in selection should know the highlights of employment law. The appendix at the end of this chapter should be helpful here.

Figure 3.2   Summary Evaluation, Criteria, and Data Sources

Position _____   **Applicant** _____

Criteria	Application, References	Portfolio	Videotape	Unit Plan	Teacher-Made Tests	Parent Letter	Interview
Reading research		X					X
Apply reading		X	X	X			X
Child development	X	X	X	X	X		X
Individual learning		X	X	X	X		X
Assess learning		X	X	X	X		X
Communicate	X	X	X	X		X	X
Coach soccer	X	X					X

STRATEGIES TO USE IN THE MIDDLE STAGE

Now the committee is ready to move into the more active middle stage.

Conduct the Applicant Screening

The first task in the middle stage is to screen out those who do not seem to meet the basic requirements, therefore not meriting a careful review. The goal here is to reduce the initial pile to three to five finalists. One efficient way is to sort all applications into three piles, coding each with a 3 (interview), 2 (hold), or 1 (reject). Once you have done a rough sorting based on your criteria, you should review all the 3s, then all the 2s, and finally all the 1s to be sure that your initial judgment is sound. File the 1s, hold the 2s, and arrange to interview the 3s. Figure 3.3 suggests what to look for in the screening process.

Use Structured Forms to Evaluate Processes and Work Products

You should find the forms provided here helpful in evaluating some of the processes and work products. Figure 3.4 illustrates a form you might use in assessing the portfolio. Figure 3.5 suggests how you might evaluate the candidate's videotape. Figure 3.6 shows criteria that can be used in evaluating a unit plan. Figure 3.7 suggests how a teacher-made test could be assessed. And Figure 3.8 offers some criteria that can be used in evaluating a parent letter.

Check the Finalists' Records for Accuracy

The members of the committee should divide the job of checking the finalists' applications for accuracy. Several checks are crucial. First, check the experience record by calling recent employers. Why did the candidate leave? What did the supervisor really think of the candidate? What were the dates of employment? What was his or her attendance record?

Next, check the educational record. Is the applicant a graduate of a standard or alternative program? What is the reputation of either? What were the dates of enrollment? What degree was awarded and when? What was the grade point average? Did the candidate actually participate in the activities claimed?

Check with the police in the town or city where the applicant last lived. Are there any major offenses? Are there any allegations of child abuse? Finally, check with the references to be sure that their written statements are not camouflaged with the polite language of the recommendation letter.

(Text continues on page 26)

Figure 3.3   Reminders in Screening Applications

Position _____   **Applicant** _____

1. Check for appearance of application, noting any misspelled words.

2. Check education. Emphasize degree earned, date awarded, and institution. Note any alternative programs—and any special workshops.

3. Check experience in teaching and related fields. Note if education and experience dates add up.

4. Check certification—state issuing, type.

5. Check references—are they appropriate? Does the language suggest that there may be problems here?

6. Keep in mind and check for two criteria:

   Knows child development

   Can use alternative forms of assessment

7. Other factors—any other indicators of quality?

Recommendation:

   _____ 3   Excellent: Interview

   _____ 2   Good to very good: Hold for further review

   _____ 1   Fair to poor: Reject

Comments:

Reviewer_____ Date_____

Figure 3.4   Portfolio Assessment

Check portfolio for these criteria and evaluate accordingly.

Criteria	Evaluation
1. Demonstrates knowledge of reading research	_____
2. Can apply research knowledge in planning and teaching	_____
3. Demonstrates knowledge of child development	_____
4. Facilitates learning of all students; individualizes learning where appropriate	_____
5. Can use alternative forms of assessment	_____

Figure 3.5   Evaluating the Videotape

The major strategy here is to focus on student learning. Rather than viewing for a specific teaching skill, watch for these signs that learning is or is not taking place. Use the following codes: 3, nearly all students show this evidence; 2, about one-half to two-thirds show this evidence; and 1, few students show this evidence. Place the appropriate code number after each criterion.

Learning Indicators	Evaluation
1. Students are using texts of appropriate difficulty.	_____
2. Student verbal responses indicate that all understand and appreciate text.	_____
3. Students are reading texts appropriate for their developmental level.	_____
4. Students' nonverbal communication suggests that all are involved with and understand texts.	_____
5. Students understand teacher directions and use teacher feedback.	_____
6. Students are guided through the learning process with appropriate scaffolding	_____

Figure 3.6   Evaluating the Unit Plan

Criteria	Evaluation
1. Unit plan shows application of knowledge of reading research.	_____
2. Unit plan is appropriate in terms of child development.	_____
3. Unit plan includes provisions for individualizing learning.	_____
4. Unit plan includes provisions for using alternative assessments.	_____
5. Unit plan is written clearly, correctly, and effectively.	_____

Figure 3.7   Evaluating Teacher-Made Tests

Criteria	Evaluation
1. Does the test reflect a knowledge of child development?	_____
2. Does the test make provisions for individual differences?	_____
3. Does the test deal specifically with the skills and knowledge taught?	_____
4. Does the test have clear directions?	_____
5. Does the test provide appropriate opportunities for the student to demonstrate learning?	_____

Figure 3.8   Evaluation of the Parent Letter

Criteria	Evaluation
1. Does the parent letter have a supportive tone?	_____
2. Does the letter make clear its purpose?	_____
3. Is the letter written correctly and effectively?	_____
4. Is the letter constructive?	_____

If you detect errors, such as a date of graduation, raise the issue in the interview. If you detect a major error (such as an employer who does not exist) or several minor errors, put the applicant in the "hold" pile.

Arrange for and Conduct the Interview

The applicant interview is a very useful tool in the selection process. However, the research indicates that principals misuse the interview (see Mertz & McNeely, 2001). The following are common mistakes made by principals:

- They make a decision based on the initial impression made by the applicant.
- That impression is typically shaped by the mental stereotype of the candidate they hope to hire.
- They ask different questions of several candidates, lacking a basis for comparison.
- They tend to look for a candidate who will fit in with the school as it is, rather than seeing the hiring process as a reform strategy.

If the interview is conducted skillfully, it can provide information relative to the criteria you have set, as indicated in the matrix and in Figure 3.9.

Figure 3.9 Suggestions for Interviewers

1. Help the applicant feel at ease with a warm welcome.

2. Review the purpose of the interview.

3. Phrase questions in a form that focuses on past behaviors.

4. Rate responses 3, 2, and 1. (3 is highest)

5. Do not ask questions that could be interpreted as discriminatory.

6. Conclude the interview by thanking the candidate and explaining what will happen next.

Criteria	Rating	Comments
1. Knows reading research		
2. Can apply research knowledge		
3. Knows, applies child development		
4. Facilitates learning, individualizing		
5. Assesses learning		
6. Communicates effectively		
7. Coaches soccer		

Some of the suggestions need special explanations. First, experts in personnel interviewing and education recommend the use of *behavior-based interviewing* (Clement, 2000; Green, 1996). Behavior-based interviewing (BBI) is based on the research that the best predictor of future performance is past performance. Therefore, you should ask about past performance, using forms such as these.

- Tell us about a time when you were able to individualize learning.
- Describe a unit that you have written.
- Tell us about how you applied the research on phonics.
- How has your prior experience changed or confirmed your thinking?
- How do you organize and deliver the reading program?
- What strategies do you use to calm a difficult parent?

The other critical reminder is not to ask questions that could be interpreted as discriminatory with respect to age, gender, race, national origin, or religion. Here are some examples of questions that could get you into trouble.

- Does your religion permit you to work on Saturdays?
- Is your wife a teacher?
- What kind of name is "Glatthorn"?
- What year did you get your doctorate?

Candidates from alternative programs may pose special problems at the interview since they do not have a broad experiential knowledge base to draw from. First, you will need to make special arrangements to make a video of their teaching. If possible, they should be requested to have a lesson they taught as a student teacher or intern. If that is not possible, arrange for a group of their colleagues to pose as students. Also in the interview, instead of asking about specific teaching strategies, inquire about their beliefs and attitudes about teaching, discipline, and diversity.

STRATEGIES TO USE IN THE END STAGE

Now you should be ready to conclude the process. Enter the ratings on the matrix, add them up, and then take a holistic perspective by answering this question:

Which applicant is best for our students?

You should contact your first choice by telephone, congratulating him or her, and checking to be sure that the applicant accepts the position. Then call the other two finalists, expressing your thanks for their applying and wishing them continued success.

Committee members could be responsible for contacting the finalists. Before making contact with candidates, check local district policies to see if your district has procedures that prevent contact with candidates. Once each finalist has been informed by phone, notify all applicants of the final decision in writing.

APPENDIX: OVERVIEW OF EMPLOYMENT LAW[1]

Employers need to learn employment law terminology to protect themselves from litigation. Below are a few definitions to help clarify some of the more critical areas of employment law. When there are specific questions about employment law, it is wise to always seek legal advice.

Affirmative Action

Affirmative action usually does not involve setting specific quotas but rather general goals to increase the numbers of minorities and women in specific positions. Affirmative action is lawful if ordered by a court to remedy past discrimination. Affirmative action may also be required of certain federal contractors. The Office of Federal Contract Compliance Programs monitors compliance with such affirmative obligations. Voluntary affirmative action programs may be upheld where there has been past discrimination and where the plan is limited in time and scope.

The Americans With Disabilities Act

The Americans With Disabilities Act prohibits discrimination against a qualified person with a disability with regard to recruiting and advertising, application procedures, hiring, advancement, discharge, compensation, training, benefits, and social events. An applicant or employee is qualified for employment if, with or without a reasonable accommodation, the applicant or employee can perform the essential functions of the job and can satisfy the requisite skills, education, experience, and job-related requirements. The Equal Employment Opportunity Commission (EEOC) regulation and interpretive guidelines provide some guidance as to what constitutes an essential function and when an accommodation is reasonable. It is best to interpret essential functions and reasonable accommodations broadly.

Title VII of the Civil Rights Acts of 1964

Title VII prohibits employers from hiring, dismissing, or making other employment decisions based on race, color, religion, sex, or national origin. In 1972, this act was amended to apply to public as well as private employers.

Fair Labor Standards Act

This act ensures that employers must meet federally mandated minimum wage and overtime standards and must maintain specified wage and hour records.

Harassment

Sexual harassment is a form of sex discrimination that violates federal, state, and most local laws. Sexual harassment can take two forms. The first, quid pro quo, occurs when a supervisor conditions the granting of some economic benefit on subordinates providing sexual favors or punishes the subordinate for not providing such favors. The second, hostile work environment, occurs when supervisors and/or coworkers create an atmosphere so infused with unwelcome sexually oriented or otherwise sexually hostile conduct that an employee's reasonable comfort level or ability to perform is undermined.

Quotas

A quota is a fixed, inflexible percentage or number of positions that an employer agrees or decides can be filled only by members of a certain minority group. Quotas are a form of reverse discrimination and are strictly scrutinized by the courts for reasonableness and necessity. Quotas are almost always illegal.

Age Discrimination in Employment Act

The Age Discrimination in Employment Act prohibits discrimination against an individual based on age with regard to hiring, discharging, compensation, terms, conditions, or privileges of employment or other actions that adversely affect the individual's status as an employee.

NOTE

1. Source: Pitt County (NC) Schools Interview Manual.

PART II

The General Strategies

Designing Your Own Model of Faculty Development

Even if you recruit and select highly qualified teachers, you will still need to facilitate their professional development. Even good teachers need to continue to grow, as new challenges present themselves and new research illuminates the science of teaching. This chapter presents an overview of a differentiated model that responds to the individual needs of teachers while saving some administrator time. Developed by Glatthorn some twenty years ago, the model was revised through an analysis of schools' experience in using the model. (See Glatthorn, 1997, for a comprehensive review of the model and Jailall, 1998, for a study of its impact.) Subsequent chapters explain in depth how the differentiated model can be used to work for teachers with special needs.

The basic premise of the differentiated model is a simple one: teachers vary significantly in their competence and professional development and thus can benefit from a supervisory approach that respects and responds to those differences. Most supervisory systems, on the other hand, seem to rest upon a belief that some form of clinical supervision should be provided to all—struggling beginners, marginally competent experienced teachers, and expert teachers.

HOW DIFFERENTIATED SUPERVISION WORKS

Each school system is encouraged to develop its own homegrown version of the model, with substantial and continuing input from teachers, administrators, and supervisors. In general, however, it operates as follows.

Required Processes

All teachers are to be involved in two types of developmental experiences: informal observations and staff development.

Informal Observations

The informal observations are brief "drop-in" visits by peers, administrators, and supervisors. Principals especially are encouraged to block in and protect an hour each day for these five- to ten-minute visits; thus, they are able to observe twenty to thirty teachers each week. These informal observations serve several administrative purposes. They enable the principal to give the teacher timely praise; they serve as a "distant early warning" system, alerting the observer to developing problems; they increase the visibility of the principal; and they provide one means for monitoring the curriculum. From the teacher's perspective, they serve to reduce the sense of isolation that most teachers experience and convey to the teacher the message that the classroom matters. Data from the informal observations should not be used in evaluating teachers since the visits are brief and the observations somewhat unsystematic.

In making an informal observation, the observer should make a brief scan of the entire room, giving special attention to the nature and extent of student learning. Here are some signs that maximum learning is *not* taking place for a particular student:

- Fussing with books and pens
- Annoying other students
- Talking with other students
- Giving a wrong answer
- Asking irrelevant questions
- Not following the teacher's directions

The observer should then estimate the approximate percentage of students who seem not to be learning. The observer should then note the teacher's behavior.

If the informal observation suggests that there might be a problem, then the observer should make a brief note, similar to this one:

10/14. 2 period. Sanchez. US history. Teacher sitting at desk. Asks the names of New England colonies. No one volunteers. About 25 percent of students off task.

Some principals tell their teachers that the informals operate under the assumption that no news is good news. If the teacher has had no feedback from the principal by the end of 48 hours, he or she can assume that there is no problem. If there might be a problem, then the principal should follow up with a brief note asking the teacher to stop in for an informal discussion. However, other experienced principals who use informals believe that feedback is crucial. Therefore, they take pains to ensure that every informal observation is followed by some type of feedback, even if only a brief written note: "Liked the small group activity—everyone active."

Staff Development

All teachers also are involved in *staff development*, which designates professional development opportunities provided in-house to groups of teachers. The staff development is seen as a keystone in the differentiated model since it serves as a cohesive force in what otherwise might be a fragmented faculty. Quality staff development, as identified by Sparks (1995) and Darling-Hammond (1997), plays a critical role in teacher development and school improvement. Chapter 5 provides greater detail about a quality staff development program.

Evaluation Options

Two evaluation tracks are provided—intensive evaluation and standard evaluation. Novice teachers and marginal tenured teachers experience an intensive evaluation since critical career choices and faculty quality are at stake. The intensive process uses several data sources: multiple observations by trained evaluators; analysis of student gain scores; assessment of such teacher work samples as plans for teaching, tests, and record books; and anecdotal reports of the performance of administrative duties. Some school systems have added parent assessments and student ratings.

The standard evaluation involves a pro forma compliance with state and district policies. The principal makes the minimum number of observations and signs the form since it is assumed that the rest of the faculty have demonstrated a satisfactory level of competence. If policies permit it, such personnel are exempt altogether from the evaluation process.

School systems have developed their own variations of this basic evaluation model. Some use a four-track system: novices, marginal tenured teachers, competent tenured teachers, and teachers identified for dismissal. Most systems provide for flexible assignments to the several tracks; thus, a novice teacher who demonstrates competence would be reassigned to the standard option. Some school systems use a cohort system: each year, one-fourth of all tenured teachers experience intensive evaluation; the rest are on the standard track. After four years, the cycle is repeated. Stiggins and

Duke (1988) recommend a three-track system: an accountability track based on performance standards for all nontenured teachers every year and for competent tenured teachers every three or four years, an assistance system for tenured teachers who seem to be deficient in performance standards, and a professional development system driven by individual growth goals for competent tenured teachers when they are not on the accountability system.

Supervisory Options

The supervisory options somewhat parallel the evaluation choices.

Intensive Development

Novices and marginal tenured teachers are provided with *intensive development*, which is Glatthorn's term for a very systematic and intensive use of clinical supervision. In this option, those who are experiencing intensive evaluation also participate in intensive development. The supervisor provides several cycles of the following services: taking-stock conference, diagnostic observation (a broad scan of all behaviors), diagnostic feedback, focused observation (a close examination of one critical aspect of performance), focused feedback, skill coaching, and knowledge development. While obviously a time-consuming process, in the long run, it requires less of the supervisor's time since it is provided only to a small number of teachers.

Cooperative Development

All competent experienced teachers are encouraged to participate in cooperative development, in which teams of teachers work together toward a common goal. Most districts find that this mode works better if it is based on an existing team structure, such as grade-level teams or subject-centered departments. The team can use several strategies to develop their knowledge and skill: action research, curriculum development, peer supervision and coaching, professional dialogs (structured discussion of current educational issues), and the development of instructional materials, such as materials that facilitate the use of the Internet. The cooperative teams are encouraged to link all their efforts to school improvement. To ensure that the cooperative work is being taken seriously, the principal needs to monitor progress, without being intrusive.

Self-Directed Development

Experienced competent teachers who find the cooperative approach too time-consuming may choose to work on their own in a self-directed model. This process is relatively simple: the teacher identifies one significant goal directly related to student achievement, establishes a plan to achieve that goal, takes the actions necessary for goal achievement, and evaluates progress at the end of the school year. The supervisor plays only a facilitative role. While the self-directed approach is less time-consuming than the cooperative mode, it seems to be effective only when feedback systems are built into the model since professional growth seems to be facilitated with professional feedback.

Many school systems permit experienced competent teachers to use cooperative or self-directed development as a substitute for teacher evaluation.

EVALUATION OF THE DIFFERENTIATED SYSTEM

Jailall (1998) used surveys and interviews to assess how school systems using differentiated supervision evaluated its effects. His study was based on a triangulation of data sources obtained through surveys, follow-up interviews, and review of written materials provided by the 28 responding school systems. The study showed that differentiated supervision approaches were successful in responding to and respecting the different needs of the various categories of teachers. Almost all of the respondents reported that their self-directed development option was highly effective or moderately effective in improving teacher performance. More than three-fourths of the schools using cooperative professional development believed it was highly effective or moderately effective in improving teacher performance.

The cooperative professional development options available involved such activities as planning, studying, developing materials, holding dialogs, and mentoring. The self-directed options available included options for the teacher's own professional growth, staff development, mentoring others, and developing the curriculum.

One overriding factor cited was that both self-directed development and cooperative professional development responded to the individual interests of teachers by providing options that teachers wanted to pursue, such as serving as instructional leaders or serving on curriculum committees, instead of meeting for observations and conferences. Teacher time for planning and training, as well as support in the form of materials and tuition reimbursement, helped improve teacher motivation and contributed to the differentiated approaches being effective. The support of the teachers union was also a contributing factor.

Of the differentiated supervision programs, 46 percent were in existence for one to three years, 32 percent for four to six years, and 21 percent for more than six years. The fact that almost half of the programs emerged within the past one to three years may be an indication that differentiated supervision is gaining ground as a supervisory model.

The factors accounting for the success of cooperative professional development options of the differentiated supervision programs were as follows, according to respondents: Programs were developed with teacher input (68 percent), program designs were effective (64 percent), teachers were highly motivated (57 percent), districts supported the programs (54 percent), highly qualified leadership was provided at the school level (46 percent), adequate resources were provided (46 percent), teachers were mature and skilled (43 percent), and school cultures supported the program (39 percent).

The factors accounting for the success of self-directed development options in the differentiated supervision program were as follows, according to respondents: Programs were developed with teacher input (86 percent), the district supported the program (79 percent), highly qualified leadership was provided at the school level (69 percent), teachers were mature and skilled (68 percent), the school culture supported the program (61 percent), program designs were effective (54 percent), teachers were highly motivated (39 percent), and adequate resources were provided (39 percent).

Only one system reported lack of success in their cooperative professional development model, citing barriers such as inadequate planning, lack of union support, and inadequate time committed to the program.

This evaluation of the differentiated supervision model suggests that teachers value the opportunity to be involved in a growth model that offers flexibility in helping them meet their professional development needs. Moreover, the study suggests that the differentiated supervision model enables teachers to choose growth opportunities consistent with their specific needs and status. Differentiated supervision seems to be a viable model capable of addressing the needs of novice teachers, tenured teachers with problems, and competent tenured teachers. The challenge of schools and systems is to develop their own homegrown model that responds to their special needs.

DEVELOPING A HOMEGROWN DIFFERENTIATED MODEL

To build support for the model and to ensure that the system responds to local needs, each school system should develop its own variation of the differentiated model. A district task force should be appointed to develop

Figure 4.1 Guidelines for Developing Homegrown Differentiated Models

The issues to be resolved are listed, followed by a recommendation based on the experience of schools using the model successfully.

1. *Should there be one system for the entire school system, or should each school develop its own?* The school system should develop systemwide guidelines, with each school developing its own model, within those guidelines.

2. *Should an entire faculty be divided into four cohorts, with each cohort experiencing intensive development once every four years, or should choices and assignments be made each year?* Both systems seem to work well.

3. *How should novice teachers or teachers new to the school be assigned?* They should be assigned to the intensive track until they have demonstrated competence.

4. *How should other teachers be assigned to the intensive development and evaluation track?* Any teacher should be assigned who, in the most recent summative evaluation, did not demonstrate mastery of all the necessary skills.

5. *May the principal veto a teacher's preferences about assignment?* While principals are encouraged to respect teachers' preferences, they may assign them to another track if they believe it is in the students' best interests to do so.

6. *May a teacher be assigned to more than one track?* Yes. For example, a teacher might be assigned to the intensive track but might also request assignment to the cooperative development track.

7. *If developmental goals are used in the self-directed or cooperative track, how many goals should be required?* One major goal is recommended.

8. *Should all goals be directly related to student learning?* Yes.

systemwide guidelines, to ensure a measure of standardization. Then each school should develop its own model, following the districtwide guidelines. Figure 4.1 identifies the issues that might be covered by the guidelines and makes recommendations based on the experience of schools that have used the model successfully.

Implementing a Quality Staff Development Program for All Teachers

All teachers should be involved in staff development, regardless of their preparation, experience, and quality. This chapter will help you by first defining the term, providing background information about staff development, suggesting models for your consideration, and explaining research-based strategies for implementing the models in an effective manner.

DEFINING THE CONCEPT OF STAFF DEVELOPMENT

It is first important to define the term *staff development* since it is used in often confusing ways. As the term is used here, it is defined as follows:

> *Staff development* includes organized training programs provided for groups of faculty and offered by the school system or the school. Two elements are crucial. First, staff development is presented to groups of faculty, to distinguish it from the individual services of supervision. Second, the programs are offered by the school system or the school, in contrast to graduate courses offered by a university. Of course, many effective staff development programs have been the result of collaborative school/university activities.

UNDERSTANDING THE BACKGROUND
OF STAFF DEVELOPMENT

Staff development has experienced a metamorphosis over the past two decades. Understanding those changes can provide a needed perspective.

Earlier Models

Just a few decades ago, staff development emphasized programs in which each educator received the same staff development at the same time with no follow-up. Typically, an "expert" was brought in to speak to teachers about a predetermined topic. Learning happened in isolation for each teacher. These traditional methods of staff development have been evident in schools for many decades. There has been little research that this type of staff development is effective for school improvement or teacher change. This type of delivery method is still evident in some staff development programs.

During the 1990s

During the 1990s, districts and schools moved to more teacher-friendly staff development models. Among others, Fullan (2001) recommended that the concept of staff development should be expanded to include learning while doing and learning from doing. Many of these staff development models are built around the principle that professional development is essential to school development and should be primarily school focused. While district-based workshops may be used at times, school-based professional development has become more prevalent. Staff development at the school level can be in the form of study groups, action research, peer coaching, and collegial study. This approach to staff development contrasts starkly with traditional staff development. When teachers become part of school-based staff development, they are found to be more likely to change their teaching practice (McLaughlin & Talbert, 1993).

The Present Picture

Currently, staff development has expanded to another level of impact. The need for schools to be productive is coupled with high-stakes accountability. The Goals 2000: Educate America Act included a goal that called for "teachers to have access to the professional development necessary to prepare students for the 21st century" (Goals 2000, n.d., p. 36).

In 2000, public school teachers were surveyed about their participation in staff development and their perceptions about the link between staff development and improved student learning. Eighty percent of teachers were most likely to have participated in professional development that focused on state or district curriculum and performance statements. This was followed by 74 percent who had professional development on the integration of educational technology into the grade or subject taught, 72 percent who had in-depth study in the subject area of the main teaching assignment, 72 percent who had staff development of new teaching strategies, and 62 percent who had staff development on student performance assessment. Sixty-two percent of new teachers had participated in staff development on classroom management, while 39 percent of experienced teachers participated (National Center for Education Statistics, 2001).

In the same 2000 survey, 18 percent of the teachers linked staff development activities to school improvement. Only 10 percent of the teachers reported follow-up reflection activities with other teachers on staff development, while 24 percent stated that administrators did not follow up on the staff development at the school level. Only 12 percent stated the staff development improved their teaching (National Center for Education Statistics, 2001). These 5,000-plus surveyed teachers clearly reveal that staff development must move to a more purpose-driven model. By having a very clear goal, staff development begins to have purpose (Williams, 1993). Mix this with individualized methods of delivery based on the needs of the group and you have staff development of the twenty-first century.

The Emerging Future

As of this writing, one can see the outlines of an emerging future for staff development. That emerging future has perhaps best been discerned in two very helpful sources. Sparks and Hirsh (1997) have noted several significant trends (the most important of which are paraphrased from their work as follows).

- From piecemeal improvement approaches to staff development driven by a strategic plan
- From district-based to school-based programs
- From training conducted in settings far removed from the job to many forms of job-embedded development
- From individual development attempted in isolation from organizational development to individual development promoted in the context of organizational development
- From an emphasis on adult needs to a concern for student outcomes
- From knowledge transmitted by so-called experts to knowledge developed by and shared with teachers

- From a focus on general teaching skills to a combination of generic and subject-specific skills
- From staff development perceived as a frill to staff development seen as an essential component

The second useful resource is the list of standards promulgated by the National Staff Development Council (2001), paraphrased in Figure 5.1. These two resources can be the focus of faculty discussion and review. Once reviewed and revised, they can then become criteria for judging your own program.

Figure 5.1   Standards for Staff Development

Context

1. Organizes staff into learning communities

2. Is guided by leaders who emphasize improvement

3. Is supported by adequate resources

Processes

4. Uses student data to determine needs

5. Uses multiple data sources

6. Emphasizes research

7. Uses appropriate learning strategies

8. Is based on knowledge about human learning

9. Emphasizes collaboration skills

10. Emphasizes need for all students to learn in a supportive environment that emphasizes high expectations for all

11. Deepens teachers' content knowledge

12. Develops skills for family involvement

SOURCE: Paraphrased from the National Staff Development Council (2001).

CHOOSING AN APPROPRIATE MODEL OF STAFF DEVELOPMENT

Before examining the research on effective delivery of staff development programs, it would help to see the big picture by considering models of staff development. Several models have been offered by experts in the field. For example, Gall and Vojtek (1994) identify these six models: expert presenter, clinical supervision, skill training, action research, organization development, and change process.

By reviewing the considerable literature on staff development and by examining our own experience in designing and implementing numerous staff development programs, we have been able to identify four major models that are more directly linked with developments in the school. The four are summarized in Figure 5.2.

Figure 5.2 Staff Development Models

Model	Typical Agendas
Model 1: Learning	• Adult learning • Psychomotor learning • Science learning • Language learning and reading • Math learning • Esthetic learning, creativity
Model 2: Faculty development	• Assessing present skills • Developing a knowledge base • Using peer coaching • Using student feedback
Model 3: School improvement	• Continuous improvement • Focused curriculum • Conveying high expectations • Safe, orderly environment • Parent involvement
Model 4: Curriculum alignment	• Scope, sequence • Organizing units • Long-term plans • Aligning tested, taught

Model 1 is a learning-centered model, where the focus is on the major types of school learning. Observe that the program is structured so that each type of learning is given a comprehensive treatment in one or more sessions. While some schools might want the entire faculty to participate in all sessions, most schools would begin with an overview session on the nature of learning in general, presented to the entire faculty. Faculty would then attend additional sessions that related directly to the subjects they teach.

Model 1 would be implemented when the principal and other leaders believe that teachers in general are ignoring essential principles of learning. A caution in adopting Model 1 is that the sessions might become too theoretical: presenters should ensure that each session includes time for discussion of the implications for teaching.

Model 2 focuses on teacher development. It would be used in conjunction with the implementation of a differentiated supervision program. A faculty might decide to adopt Model 2 when several new teachers have been added to the faculty or when school leaders believe that teachers in general need to make significant improvements in their teaching.

Model 3 is a school improvement model. It would be implemented when the faculty have decided to embark on a schoolwide improvement program. Each topic would be developed in depth and presented in a manner that resulted in informed action. Here, for example, is how the component of "high expectations" might be developed.

1. High expectations—what they are and why they are important

2. Conveying high expectations by the language we use

3. Conveying high expectations by our classroom actions

4. Being sensitive to the problem of unrealistic expectations

In this model, the staff development session would be followed by a peer coaching experience, when teachers would give each other feedback about their success in conveying high expectations.

Model 4 is a curriculum alignment model, adopted when a new curriculum has been implemented or when classroom observations indicate that teachers are experiencing difficulty in operationalizing the curriculum. Most of these sessions would engage teachers in producing curriculum materials that would assist in their planning, as explained more fully in Chapter 11.

Some principals might see a need for mixing the models. The only caution here is that mixing the models might result in a lack of focus and connectedness.

Prior to an administrator or school improvement team choosing one of the four staff development models, the decision makers must first analyze the needs of their faculty and students. Finding the balance between the needs of the faculty and student achievement can be done through surveys, focus groups, observation, or interviews. In addition, the analysis of school test data, feedback from students and parents, and other data sources will allow the team or administrators to determine the appropriate model. All four models are built around the central focus of higher student achievement based on the knowledge, skills, and dispositions of the teachers.

The models for staff development provide administrators with a structure to determine which type of staff development matches the needs of their faculty. The models are developmental in nature, moving from a knowledge-based model to more of an evaluative model through school improvement.

IMPLEMENTING STAFF DEVELOPMENT EFFECTIVELY

Regardless of which model is chosen, school leaders should implement the programs effectively. Here a body of research can be helpful in ensuring successful implementation. The recommendations listed in Figure 5.3 represent a synthesis of several useful sources (see Darling-Hammond &

Figure 5.3 Effective Staff Development Progress

1. Center on critical activities of teaching and learning (planning, evaluating, developing curriculum), emphasizing job-embedded learning. Keep the focus on student learning.

2. Grow from investigations and involve teachers as action researchers.

3. Are built on substantial professional discourse that fosters analysis and communication about practices among colleagues.

4. Reflect sound principles of adult learning.

5. Honor the individual learning styles and needs of the professional educator.

6. Allow for and foster reflection and mindfulness.

7. Are supported by adequate resources.

8. Recognize that teachers are at various stages of readiness for new programs and approaches and respond individually to staff development.

9. Provide sufficient time for follow-up and collaboration; do not interfere with teachers' other responsibilities.

10. Provide opportunities for teachers to develop knowledge in depth about the subjects they teach and means of helping students acquire that knowledge.

11. Are supported with reasonable incentives, such as credits, reimbursement of expenses, and released time.

12. Are structured with clear, specific, and meaningful objectives, with programs designed to meet those objectives.

13. Are planned, developed, and implemented by teachers.

14. Are evaluated systematically.

McLaughlin, 1995; Gall & Vojtek, 1994; Sparks, 1995). While these suggestions are based on numerous well-designed studies, keep in mind that they may not apply to your school and your faculty in all cases.

PUTTING IT ALL TOGETHER

As a means of integrating and exemplifying the recommendations presented in this chapter, the chapter concludes with an extended example showing how one school designed and conducted a staff development program. As you read this example, consider how you might modify it for use in a school you know.

The prior experience of teachers at Jones Middle School has left them with negative feelings about staff development. In the past, they have been required to attend after-school meetings in which an external expert lectured to them about the principal's new bandwagon. The most recent was a boring presentation on brain-based teaching. The new principal, Sue Walker, has decided to wipe the slate clean and develop a different model.

She decides that staff development will be the responsibility of the School Improvement Team since that group seems to work together well and has done an excellent job managing change. In an early discussion, two team members raised the issue of teacher planning, noting that few teachers did any unit planning, despite some literature arguing that daily planning without unit planning left students with a fragmented view of the subject. Those two advocates of unit planning suggested that the school invite an expert in unit planning at the elementary level. A heated discussion ensued, with some teachers arguing that unit planning at the secondary level was quite different from the elementary approach.

Principal Walker suggests that they study the issue. She informs the district assistant superintendent of their plans to gather data and then use the results to plan a series of staff development sessions on unit planning. The assistant superintendent supports the plan, asking to be kept informed about progress, since the district leadership team has expressed an interest in improving teacher planning. Walker works with the team in designing a simple survey that asks teachers about their planning approach. The team decides to use its own model of curriculum development and alignment.

The chair of the team speaks to the faculty about the team's tentative proposal, noting that the team would like each teacher who uses unit planning to give the team an example of his or her unit planning. The team ensures the faculty that the units will be analyzed only to make a needs assessment, not to evaluate the teacher. The analysis of the data indicates that only 20 percent of the teachers report that they use unit planning. The unit plans submitted seem very sketchy and poorly designed.

Two issues arise in the team's early discussion: Should we emphasize curriculum integration, and should we require all teachers to participate, even those who are using unit planning? To examine the first issue, the team requests Walker to work with a university faculty member to review the research. The review indicates that the early research strongly supported curriculum integration; however, more recent studies raise a concern that too much integration slights subject matter knowledge. The team decides to put integration on the back burner. On the second issue, the team recommends to the principal that she require all teachers to attend since part of the time will be used to develop the school's approach to unit development.

The team then plans a series of staff development sessions, to be held on ten Friday mornings, with teachers released for the first two hours of each Friday. They send the following list of session topics and activities to the faculty, asking for faculty input on these first six sessions.

1. *Unit planning: pros and cons.* This first session will feature a presentation by two of the teachers—one who uses unit planning and one who does only daily planning. The presentations will be fifteen minutes each, followed by small group discussion. The faculty will be organized by teaching teams. The teams decide that for the first year, unit planning will be encouraged but not mandated.

2. *Developing our unit development model.* Prior to this session, faculty will receive a two-page summary of Glatthorn's unit development model. Faculty will again meet in small groups, by teams, to review and critique the model. Each team will submit to the school improvement team a summary of its concerns and questions. The team reviews these reports and uses them to develop the school's process model. Teachers will be encouraged to test the model in their unit planning but will not be required to do so.

3. For the next four weeks, each instructional team will work together during the released time to use the model to develop one unit. They will note in a special report their problems and successes in using the process model. The school improvement team uses those reports to revise the process model.

The team decides that it is time for an evaluation of these sessions. It surveys the teachers and examines the units. The teachers express a high level of satisfaction with their work, but the unit evaluation concludes that the units had interesting activities—but too many were not directly related to the unit objectives. The team decides to recommend to the principal one more session on results-oriented units.

A FINAL NOTE

Some teachers complain that, too often, staff development is a waste of time. That indictment is warranted when the programs are planned without teacher input or are presented in a manner that results in boredom and lack of attention. However, staff development at its best can be a powerful process for teacher growth and school reform.

PART III

The Specific Approaches

Developing a Quality Induction Program for New Teachers

The term *induction program* is used here with this meaning:

> A program of planned experiences designed to help teachers new to the school achieve the goal of better learning for teacher and students.

A few features of the definition should be noted. First, the induction program is a set of planned experiences, not a collection of spur-of-the-moment meetings. Second, the core of the program should be presented to all teachers new to the building, including teachers who have been teaching in some other school. Finally, induction has one main goal—better learning for teacher and students. If a given activity does not help teachers learn and, in turn, foster student learning, it is a waste of time. In accomplishing this central goal, you should keep in mind other related outcomes. One is to help the new teachers develop a sense of affiliation—an attitude of "This is my school, and I belong here." The second is to help them become socialized to the organization, understanding its values, norms of behavior, rituals, and ceremonies. Finally, the program should provide the new teacher with the support needed when things go wrong.

IMPORTANCE OF INDUCTION PROGRAMS

An effective induction program has several desirable results. From the perspective of the new teachers, it has the following benefits.

- Clear expectations of school and district
- Fewer discipline problems
- Smooth assimilation into the organization
- Less apprehension about getting help
- A feeling of acceptance
- A sense of success

From the school's perspective, an effective induction program brings to the faculty a new resource, not one more problem. One principal put it this way:

> We have a strong induction program that makes new teachers an active participant in our school improvement process. And as many of the old hands see the beginner profit from coaching, they start to change their own attitudes.

Obviously, induction programs for new teachers take both time and money. The evidence says that the gain is worth the pain.

ORGANIZATIONAL STRUCTURES NEEDED

Although some principals believe that informal "buddy" systems are more effective than structured programs, some research disputes that claim. In one comparative study, a structured program was found to be more effective than the informal approach (Klug & Salzman, 1990). Each school system should develop its own committee structure and planning processes; however, the experience of successful practitioners can provide some guidance here in answering the issues analyzed below.

The conclusions reached for each issue should be seen as recommendations for consideration.

Committees Needed

First, a comprehensive district approach to induction is needed to ensure effective and efficient coordination across district schools. This comprehensive approach should be developed by whatever committee and individual are responsible for planning all staff development for the district. Many school systems have found it helpful to use an existing "Staff Development Advisory Council" to discharge this responsibility. That council could be chaired by the director of staff development.

At the school level, whoever is chiefly responsible for instructional leadership should develop the school's induction program, with input from the School Improvement Team. In most schools, the team is chaired by the principal or the assistant principal for instruction.

The general intent in delineating these structures is to fix responsibility without adding more committees. Most schools already have too many committees.

Duration of the Program

Some leaders consider the before-school orientation meeting their "induction program." That two-day program is not sufficient. Others have developed multiyear programs. The recommendation here is to develop a flexible program for the period from August 10 to December 10 during the first year. Then evaluate what has been accomplished to determine how much additional time is needed in the second semester. At the end of May, evaluate again to determine whether a second year is needed. In some cases, a third year may be needed.

Distinguishing Teacher Development and Evaluation

Teacher development is quite different from teacher evaluation— forms used, type of observation, person in charge, and type of conference. Teachers from alternative programs especially need professional development that is supportive and nonthreatening. One solution about the person in charge issue is to have a mentor responsible for development and a school administrator for evaluation.

Released Time

The induction process is one of high demand for the inductee. Some have complained vociferously about "too many meetings and too much advice." On the other hand, if the principal tries to reduce the beginner's assignment, the more experienced teachers often complain about the supposed favoritism shown to novices. However, experts in the field believe that a lighter schedule is highly desirable. If the principal takes pains to build support among the rest of the faculty for the novice's released time program, then the complaining is less likely to occur. Also, the principal should work hard to develop a culture in which teachers work together for the common good.

Program Collaboration

Effective collaboration with local universities can be very helpful to both universities and schools. The mutual exchange of ideas and experiences broadens the outlook of both faculties.

SPECIAL NEEDS OF NEW TEACHERS

There is danger, of course, in speaking generally about new teachers' needs since they do vary significantly. However, the list shown in Figure 6.1 is a summary of the research, which can be used as the basis of a needs assessment. The results of the needs assessment can be used for program planning. Suppose, for example, that you have five new teachers. Three of the five report that they want development of Skill 5 (communicating with parents). One reports that he or she just needs to refine the skill. One claims mastery of the skill. You might well decide to offer a seminar for the first four, with the one who claims mastery assisting with the presentation.

Note first that having better discipline is almost always listed as the chief concern for new teachers. Learning how to increase student motivation is also frequently at the top of teachers' concerns. Since students are becoming increasingly diverse in today's schools, conscientious teachers are concerned with meeting their special needs. New forms of assessment must be mastered and used appropriately. New teachers are also concerned with parent communications.

While teachers from alternative programs are generally strong in content knowledge, many have problems with *pedagogical content knowledge*, the ability to make academic content available and understandable to students (see Shulman, 1987). Thus, although such a teacher may know quite a bit about the Elizabethan theater, he or she may not be able to help tenth graders make their own sense of that knowledge.

Helping students do well on state tests is becoming a greater concern for new teachers with the rise of state-imposed accountability systems. Experienced teachers report that they see state tests as just one more bureaucratic constraint (see Glatthorn & Fontana, 2000). New teachers report greater anxiety about their students' performance.

Like most teachers, the new ones on the block want appreciation, respect, encouragement, and merited praise. However, the support should never be a substitute for effective professional development. Also, new

Figure 6.1   Needs Assessment Instrument

Directions: Listed below are several areas in which most beginning teachers believe they would like additional assistance. For each area listed, circle one of these responses:

MA—I feel I have *mastered* this area.

RE—I probably need some help *refining* this area.

DE—I need help *developing* this area.

Your responses will not be used to evaluate you. They will be used to help us plan an individualized program for you.

1. Having better discipline	MA	RE	DE
2. Motivating students	MA	RE	DE
3. Adapting for individual differences	MA	RE	DE
4. Assessing student learning	MA	RE	DE
5. Communicating with parents	MA	RE	DE
6. Adapting subject matter content	MA	RE	DE
7. Helping students do well on state tests	MA	RE	DE
8. Gaining support from students, parents, administrators, colleagues	MA	RE	DE
9. Using my time wisely	MA	RE	DE

teachers report that they need time—to plan, meet, teach, and take graduate courses. Probably many had been told by misinformed critics that teaching is easy. The reality they experience is discomfiting.

Finally, new teachers report that they feel overwhelmed with all the paperwork required of them.

FEATURES OF EFFECTIVE INDUCTION PROGRAMS

You can do a better job of planning your own induction program if you can answer the question of what makes an effective program. Obviously, you will need to tailor your program to the special needs and resources of your schools, using the following discussion as a set of general guidelines. (The following features were identified by a review of the literature, chiefly the following: Klug & Salzman, 1990; Robinson, 1998; Sweeny, 2001; U.S. Department of Education, 1998; Weiss & Weiss, 1999.)

- The program is tailored to the needs of the participants. Rather than copying other programs or assuming what new teachers need, those in charge assess the needs of their clients.
- The program emphasizes learning—for both teacher and students. The ultimate goal is better student learning, and teacher learning is the best way to foster student learning.
- The program provides important information "just in time." If the first parents' meeting is scheduled for September 15, the assistance for new teachers should be offered around September 8, not August 15 or September 14.
- The program is flexible. As new teachers develop professionally and understand the school, the program becomes less intense.
- The program is collaborative. University faculty from both the teacher education department and the liberal arts units cooperate as equals in planning and delivering a high-quality induction program.
- The program emphasizes support and development, not evaluation. Evaluation is deferred and minimized until the inductee seems ready for formal evaluation.
- The program is supported by district and school administrators who value the program and provide sufficient resources for it.
- The program embodies the principles of adult learning, emphasizing the integration of sound knowledge and effective practice.
- The program emphasizes classroom observation and constructive feedback.

- The program is delivered chiefly by a highly competent mentor, who models good teaching. The mentor is given adequate released time.

SERVICES PROVIDED

The answer to the question of what makes an effective induction program is complex, best answered by understanding the planning matrix shown in Figure 6.2. Note first that the matrix lists three phases occurring during the first term, as identified by Moir (1999).

Figure 6.2   Comprehensive Induction Program

Phase	Month	District	School	Team	Individual
Anticipation	August	Opening day orientation	Opening day orientation	Planning meeting; problem solving	Set up room; meet with buddy
Anticipation	September		Leadership seminar	State testing program	Professional development with mentor
Survival	October		Leadership seminar	Team planning	Professional development; evaluation; observation
Disillusionment	November	Effective use of central staff	Leadership seminar	Curriculum development	Professional development; evaluation; observation optional
Disillusionment	December		Leadership seminar	Planning for spring term	Professional development; evaluation; observation

Anticipation probably starts during the last weeks of student teaching and continues for a month or so on the job. It is a time of high hopes and self-confidence.

Survival concerns take over. Some problems develop for which there are no easy solutions.

Disillusionment sets in as problems get worse. Now the new teacher begins to distrust and criticize the parents.

In Moir's (1999) research, the teacher's attitudes continue to change during the second term, moving from *rejuvenation*, through *reflection*, and finally to *anticipation* again.

Observe as well that the matrix shows four program levels. The district offices present an orientation program in August and a work session in November. The opening-day orientation session needs careful planning. In too many cases, the district orientation consists of long, boring speeches by such individuals as the director of food services, the transportation coordinator, and the business manager, followed by a bus tour of the community. All the while, the new teachers are worried about their schedules, their rooms, and their textbooks. In the November work session, the new teacher works with the central office staff on such issues as curriculum and testing.

The second level describes activities at the school level. A series of leadership seminars conducted by the principal gives both the new teachers and the principal an opportunity to get to know each other, air concerns, and make suggestions. One process that seems to work is to arrange schedules so that all new teachers have one lunch period in common each week. The principal can then use that time for a bag lunch in his or her office. The topics for the seminar can be identified by the principal and the new teachers in dialog.

The team plays a very important role in the induction process (see Chapter 6 for a full discussion of the team and its responsibilities). All team members meet during their preparation period to do some problem solving. The inductee plays an active role—listening, contributing, and learning.

Finally, the chart shows entries for the individual working chiefly with the mentor. Note, however, that some school systems appoint a temporary "buddy" who is expected only to answer the pressing questions of the first two weeks: How do you run the copy machine? Is there a faculty lounge? Where do I get the textbooks? That temporary assignment gives the principal some time to appoint the permanent mentor, who plays such a critical role.

USE OF TECHNOLOGY

Most schools have improved in student use of technology—but so far have not made effective use of the technology in their induction programs. The uses listed below have been culled from a rather limited body of literature and the authors' experience. (The single best source here is probably Sweeny, 2001.)

Curriculum Work

First, the mentor and the inductee can together retrieve information that will help them in their standards-based curriculum work. Almost every state Department of Education now lists its curriculum standards as part of its homepage material. Yahoo, one of the Internet service providers, has an excellent collection of curriculum standards. The educational data bank, ERIC, provides sample lesson plans and summaries of the research. Also, many state departments of education provide sample lesson plans that new teachers find helpful.

Communication

The availability of e-mail has greatly simplified communication in complex organizations. The mentor and the teacher can easily stay in touch. Teachers who are teaching in special programs may wish to keep in touch with counterparts in other schools. And chat rooms are useful in exploring educational issues.

Current Developments in Education

The Internet is an excellent way to stay abreast of educational issues. Almost every professional association now has its own homepage. For example, the Association of Supervision and Curriculum publishes its own newsletter, which does a fine job of keeping readers current about major issues. Another excellent newsletter is published by the Fordham Foundation, a conservative think tank.

Distance Learning

Many distance-learning courses are available for teachers who need additional course work to meet state requirements. Search the Internet for current information on *distance learning.*

Professional Development

The central concern of all induction programs, of course, is the professional development of the teacher-inductee. Here video has proved to be an invaluable resource. In a widely used approach, the inductee arranges to have a videotape made of one of his or her lessons. The inductee then presents the tape to the team, which gives the inductee feedback about the teaching.

While new and helpful uses of technology continue to develop, keep in mind that no technology can take the place of the human mentor.

EVALUATION OF INDUCTION PROGRAMS

Consider using a two-phase program evaluation, following the lead of Guskey (2002).

Results-Oriented Evaluation

The first phase focuses on results, asking only two questions. The first and more important question is, "Did the students make appropriate gains in their learning?" If the students have not made the gains they should have made, then the program has failed, regardless of its features. Several means can be used to assess the impact on learning. First, the students' scores on comprehensive tests can be analyzed. Second, the mentor can make systematic observations that focus on learning. Students can be surveyed to assess their perceptions of their learning. Finally, the perceptions of the teacher about learning can be assessed.

The second results-oriented question is, "Does the school retain competent faculty for at least five years of service?" As noted in Chapter 12, losing competent teachers is a consummate waste of resources. All teachers who indicate they plan to leave should be debriefed in an exit interview to determine their reasons for leaving.

Features-Oriented Evaluation

The other type of evaluation recommended here is to assess the features of the induction program, to determine to what extent it embodies the characteristics suggested by the research. The characteristics of effective programs presented earlier can be used to construct an evaluative survey, as shown in Figure 6.3.

A FINAL NOTE

The first years of working for any large organization are difficult for most professionals. An effective induction program can make the experience less painful and more satisfying.

Figure 6.3   Assessment of Program Features

The following characteristics are found in effective induction programs. From your perspective, to what extent were they found in the program you experienced?

Circle one of these responses:

    GRE to a great extent

    MOD to a moderate extent

    LIT to a little extent or not at all

Program Characteristics   *Your Rating*

The induction program . . .

1. Is tailored to the needs of new teachers	GRE	MOD	LIT
2. Emphasizes learning for all	GRE	MOD	LIT
3. Provides timely information	GRE	MOD	LIT
4. Is flexible	GRE	MOD	LIT
5. Is collaborative, including higher education	GRE	MOD	LIT
6. Emphasizes support and development	GRE	MOD	LIT
7. Is supported by district and school administrators	GRE	MOD	LIT
8. Embodies principles of adult learning	GRE	MOD	LIT
9. Emphasizes classroom observation and feedback	GRE	MOD	LIT
10. Is led and coordinated by trained mentors	GRE	MOD	LIT

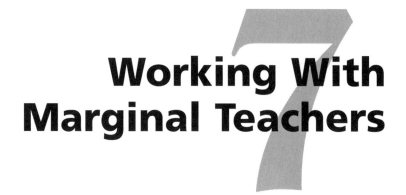

Working With Marginal Teachers

Although the discussion has thus far emphasized the major aspects of recruiting and selecting highly qualified faculty, there remains the reality of current staff who require performance improvement. It seems that every faculty has at least one marginal teacher. Therefore, this chapter examines these issues relating to the marginal teacher: defining the term and identifying the marginal teacher, developing the marginal teacher, evaluating the marginal teacher, making a final decision, and helping marginal teachers with special problems.

DEFINING THE TERM AND IDENTIFYING THE MARGINAL TEACHER

The first issue is one of definition and identification.

Definition

Several researchers have classified teachers in general and have defined the term; these typologies and definitions can assist in defining the term. Lawrence, Vachon, Leake, and Leake (1993) describe the marginal teacher as a teacher who has lost faith in the belief that every child can learn. They also suggest that there are several observable indicators that a teacher is becoming or has become marginal: number of disciplinary referrals, large percentage of student failure, and several complaints from colleagues, students, and parents. As Danielson and McGreal (2000) have analyzed the problem, marginal teachers are those who are experiencing difficulty in meeting the standards of the school system for effective teaching. According to Glickman (2002), there are four types of teachers: teacher dropouts, unfocused workers, analytical observers, and the professionals. Dropouts and unfocused workers would probably be classified as marginal.

These typologies and definitions lead us to the following synthesis:

> A marginal teacher is one who is not fully facilitating student learning and is thereby not meeting the school system's standards for effective teaching.

This definition will be used throughout the rest of this chapter.

Identification

Most school systems have formal processes for identifying marginal teachers. The following suggestions should be of help in reviewing existing processes or developing new ones.

First, the principal should be sensitive to and aware of the "distant early warning" signals that suggest a teacher is having problems.

- Classroom observations indicate little learning is taking place. A single unsatisfactory observation may be just an aberration; the second may signal trouble.
- Students achieve low scores on state tests. State tests are not perfect measures of achievement, but they can serve as signals of trouble.
- Previous administrators have made observations judged unsatisfactory. Observers will always differ about particulars, but most principals know an unsatisfactory performance when they see it.
- Supervisors have noted little improvement over the course of a year.
- Parents, students, and colleagues have complained about the teacher's performance.
- The teacher has made a large number of disciplinary referrals. Effective teachers take care of the few problems that they encounter; ineffective teachers use the principal as a disciplinary dumping ground.
- The teacher is often absent from or late to school.
- A large percentage of students have failed the course. Some marginal teachers boast of their high failure rate as a result of high standards. An effective teacher sets high standards and helps students meet them.

- Students tend not to enroll in advanced levels of the subject. Ineffective teachers of mathematics produce students who hate mathematics.

You should not jump to the conclusion that you are dealing with a marginal teacher on the basis of one indicator. Look for a pattern of behavior. Unsatisfactory observations are probably the most reliable factor.

If two or more indicators are evident, confer with the teacher. In this critical conference, review the indicators and give the teacher an opportunity to add his or her comments. Then explain in detail the assistance that will be provided and the formal evaluation that will be undertaken. This conference thus formalizes the teacher's assignment to intensive development and intensive evaluation, as explained in Chapter 4. Finally, express the hope that the teacher achieves significant improvement. Summarize the conference in a written report for the teacher with a copy for the personnel file.

With the marginal teacher assigned to the intensive evaluation and the intensive development tracks, the question arises as to which should take priority—evaluation or development. If you believe that the teacher has the potential to improve once skills have been developed, then development should take priority. However, if you feel that the marginal teacher is not likely to improve, then evaluation should take priority. In either case, the two approaches need to be coordinated closely, so that the marginal teacher is not overwhelmed.

DEVELOPING THE MARGINAL TEACHER

Most marginal teachers have common problems that make them marginal. The following suggestions should be of help.

First, develop a formal plan that specifies in detail the nature of the development program. That plan should indicate what skills will be developed, when the coaching sessions will be held, and how progress will be measured. Also be sure to specify who will be responsible for implementing the plan. This person responsible for development should probably not have an evaluative role since evaluation tends to close off discussion— and openness here is vital. Remember that the development plan should be coordinated with the evaluation plan. Figure 7.1 provides an example of one such plan.

Developing a system of planned assistance is the first step to supporting the marginal teacher. In developing and implementing the plan, you

Figure 7.1 Sample Development Plan

Teacher: Lomax

Implementer: Washburn

Skill to be developed: Maximizes use of time for learning, using appropriate routines.

Development schedule: The following schedule will be implemented flexibly, coordinated with the evaluation plan.

Topic	*Date*	*Developer*
1. Importance of time	9/16	Washburn
2. Using routines to save time	9/23	Goodbar
3. Handling transitions smoothly	9/30	Washburn

....

Assessing progress

Each training session will be followed by a focused observation to determine how effectively the teacher uses the skill.

---

may wish to keep in mind the four approaches identified by Glickman (2002): the directive-control approach, the directive-informational approach, the collaborative approach, and the nondirective approach. The approaches, while different in some manner, all describe techniques for working with teachers to improve classroom performance. Clarifying, presenting, directing, demonstrating, standardizing, and reinforcing strategies are used as approaches in directive control; the same strategies are used to develop options for teachers to choose from and commit to in the informational approach. The collaborative approach uses clarifying, listening, problem solving, and negotiating to develop a contract with the teacher. The nondirective approach uses clarifying, listening, problem solving, encouraging, and presenting to create a teacher self-plan.

The directive-control approach to working with the teacher results in an assignment for the teacher to be carried out over a designated time period. The administrator designates what the assignment will entail based on observation and data collection. The assignment is presented to the teacher in detail with criteria for improvement and a completion deadline. This approach would be effective when working with a marginal teacher who has not recognized what changes are necessary. The administrator maintains complete control over the improvement process.

The directive-informational approach, which should not be confused with the directive-control approach, allows the teacher to determine the plan for improvement. The administrator provides the teacher with suggestions for corrective action, but the ultimate decision of what to do is left to the teacher to decide. The administrator in this scenario believes that the marginal teacher has the ability to identify and implement strategies for improvement.

The collaborative approach results in development of a mutually agreed-on contract between the administrator and the teacher. The contract clearly states the structure, process, and criteria for improvement. The plan should include the views of both and be a true collaboration. They should review, revise, reject, and propose until they reach an agreement.

The last approach, nondirective, requires the administrator to serve as a facilitator for the teacher and to refrain from imposing any structure or direction to the teacher. The administrator must accept the teacher's right and responsibility to make the final decision and work toward a self-plan. While the last approach is totally self-directed, it could be perceived as a loss of control by some administrators. The administrator must fully understand the role of a facilitator for this approach to have positive results.

The best plan of assistance is the plan that produces the desired results. Although most marginal teachers have similar problems, improvement strategies should be individualized and grounded in the strengths and needs of the teacher. Some marginal teachers will be capable of directing their own improvement and could be successful using the nondirective approach; others will require the full intervention as described in the directive-control approach.

The collaborative approach, which allows the greatest opportunity for the marginal teacher and the administrator to work together on the improvement plan, should be the preferred approach when possible. The approach allows for a partnership between teacher and administrator in working for improvement. The teacher and the administrator are required to communicate their desires and reach agreement. The teacher can take ownership of the plan, and the administrator does not need to be concerned about loss of control.

Also, review the development plan with district supervisors and administrators since the plan plays such a crucial role. This review should assess the development plan for its developmental soundness and conformity with the teachers' contract.

EVALUATING THE MARGINAL TEACHER

The marginal teacher also needs to be evaluated intensively. Here again a systematic plan is needed, one that is coordinated with the development plan. Schools and school districts have options in selecting an appropriate evaluation plan. The evaluation plan should clearly specify the elements that will make up the formal evaluation. The following elements are recommended.

- Evaluation observations
- Anecdotal records of the teacher's performance in carrying out administrative responsibilities
- Work samples, such as lesson plans, units, record books, and tests

The evaluation plan should also clearly indicate the dates and foci of all planned conferences, including a final evaluation conference, and clearly indicate who will be responsible for implementing the plan. Figure 7.2 shows an example of such a plan.

The evaluation plan should be carefully reviewed to ensure that it complies with the teachers' contract and provides adequately for due process.

Figure 7.2 Sample Evaluation Plan

Administrator responsible: Smithson, principal

Dates	Observations	Conferences
9/3		Taking stock
9/17	Reading	Feedback
9/24	Mathematics	Feedback
10/15		Work sample evaluation
11/1		Taking stock
4/18		Final evaluation

A few comments about the plan might be helpful here. First, note that the principal is responsible for carrying out the evaluation plan. She wisely decides to observe Williams teaching reading and mathematics since the principal wants to be sure that she has a representative sample of the teacher's performance—and elementary teachers differ in their teaching from subject to subject. A high school principal would achieve the same goal by observing the teacher's first-period class and the last class of the day.

The teaching portfolio is a method of enabling the teacher to assemble evidence of performance and to present work samples in a systematic manner (see Green & Smyser, 1996). The chief drawback with the portfolio in evaluating the marginal teacher is that it is entirely teacher selected. Only a rare teacher would present evidence of failure. However, the development of a teacher portfolio allows teachers to integrate all aspects of teaching (Lawrence et al., 1993).

Note also that the evaluation plan includes two "taking stock" conferences in which the principal and the teacher discuss what has been achieved and what will happen. Also note that the principal schedules a final evaluation conference, at which the overall assessment is presented. The final conference should not present the marginal teacher with any surprises.

MAKING A FINAL DECISION

In making a final decision about whether to retain or dismiss a marginal teacher, keep in mind the following guidelines.

Give significant weight to the teacher's attitudes toward such elements as the following: testing and accountability, lesson and unit planning, supervision and peer coaching, student failure, parent involvement, and professional growth. Given two teachers with approximately the same skill level, choose the one who thinks and acts more professionally.

Retain teachers who have shown improvement and seem likely to continue that growth. Also, focus on student learning, not on whether the teacher uses a given method. Retain teachers who can foster learning; release those who cannot.

Consider these options for borderline teachers:

- Instructional reassignment—different grade, different subject
- Reassignment to noninstructional role
- Medical leave of absence
- Sabbatical leave for professional growth
- Early retirement

In considering these options, keep in mind this slogan: *Students come first.* Focus on improving the teacher, not on firing him or her. In the last analysis, students must come first. Teachers must be held accountable for what they teach students. Principals should not retain the incompetent even though dismissal and loss of tenure may be personal tragedies.

HELPING MARGINAL TEACHERS
WITH SPECIAL PROBLEMS

The following snapshots have been developed to assist you in understanding that marginal teachers may vary a great deal—and that some of their problems may need strategies other than intensive help. The snapshots are composite pictures of marginal teachers with whom we have worked; they do not represent actual teachers.

There is no single right answer to these individual problems, but reflecting about them may help you identify the key issues. Consider these five questions.

1. What is the teacher's basic problem—the major difficulty that is causing the symptoms of trouble?

2. Can you as a school administrator solve or ameliorate that basic problem?

3. In what specific ways can you best help the teacher?

4. Which component of differentiated supervision would probably be most helpful?

5. All other elements being equal, is it likely that you would retain or dismiss this teacher—or offer an option?

Retired Ray

Until three years ago, Ray Reston was considered a competent team player who could always be counted on to assist in school projects and sponsor student activities. Then, three years ago, his health went down-hill. He developed Parkinson's disease, had triple bypass surgery, and continued his battle with the ravages of diabetes. His own health problems took their toll. He seemed to have little energy and was often absent because of illness. He seemed to lose interest in teaching after his wife developed an inoperable cancer. He has told colleagues that he will retire five years from now.

He uses old lesson plans, based primarily on a U.S. history text that is no longer used. He does a competent job of covering the syllabus that a colleague has prepared. His students achieve average scores on the state-administered end-of-course test, although scores have been declining of late. Students seem to act condescendingly toward him. He has always received "satisfactory" ratings from his principals. However, his teaching no longer seems satisfactory. Most of his students show signs of boredom in his classes and spend most of the class time doing seatwork. From time to time, he lectures students about "the good old days" and bemoans the weakness of present students.

Friendly Phil

Phil Johnson is thirty years old and considers himself a friend of the students, although most students do not seem to regard him as a friend. They often make humorous comments about his attempts to be young. Several parents have expressed concern because he invites students to his home for discussions of current issues and organizes bus trips to New York City. He dismisses these concerns as "foolish worries by arch conservatives." Town gossips charge him with embracing a gay lifestyle, but there have been no reports of inappropriate behavior with students. The principal has also received several parent complaints about his liberal stance on controversial issues.

The chief problem in his classes is classroom management. Even when students act disrespectful to him, he brushes off their snide remarks with a smile. He defends the disruptive climate by arguing that it is all "great discussion," although some colleagues have characterized the climate as "chaotic." He makes extensive use of cooperative learning, although observers have noted that he has no accountability strategies. Students seem to enjoy his classes because he is seen as an easy teacher who makes no demands on students. Student scores are low on the state test. His attitude toward the test is, "If you can test it, it is not worth teaching." He expresses this feeling openly, seeming to enjoy the controversy that his stance engenders.

Scholarly Sue

Sue Markle majored in history at one of the Ivy League schools. She has spoken openly about her desire to teach at the higher education level, at the present time teaching part-time at the community college. She knows the content well but has difficulty making it interesting and meaningful to students. She speaks often of "high standards," especially when administrators express concern about the large number of student failures. Each year, about one-fourth of her students fail the course and are required to make up the work in summer school.

Every class involves a 45-minute lecture, complete with transparencies. Students furiously take notes because of their fear of failure. There is no discussion. Students are also required to write a 35-page term paper, with Sue spending one full marking period teaching the term paper. Her gifted students do well on the Advanced Placement test but earn only average scores on the state test. Her colleagues believe that she is not getting better results on the state test because she spends so much time on the term paper. She defends her practice by citing the importance of teacher autonomy.

Easy Ed

Ed Watkins says he entered teaching because it offered an easy career—short school day, several holidays, and a long summer. When he thinks the principal is not listening, he boasts that he spends only fifteen minutes each night on schoolwork. He has a part-time job as a shoe salesman at the local mall. Colleagues complain that he does not do his share of the work involved in team projects.

At his request, he has been assigned to a primary grade class because he thought it would be an easy assignment. But he is having serious problems. He seems to view students as the enemy, spending most of classroom time warning, scolding, and punishing students. He blames the students and their parents and is especially critical of minority students and their families.

The second-grade curriculum emphasizes reading and mathematics. Ed seems completely unaware of how to teach reading. He uses his own version of "whole language," with students trying to read "Big Books" that are too difficult to read. His teaching of mathematics also leaves much to be desired. Most of the time is spent on whole-class instruction, with very little student participation. His students score at the bottom on state tests in reading and mathematics.

A FINAL NOTE

With the right kind of assistance and support, the marginal teacher may be able to contribute to student learning. This chapter provides school administrators with a resource to use with teachers who are not meeting the minimum performance requirements of their school or school district. Administrators should use these suggestions to guide their work with teachers who need support and guidance.

Using Self-Directed Development With Highly Qualified Teachers

Highly qualified teachers can foster their own development through a self-directed process. This chapter provides detailed information to help you understand the nature of self-directed development, analyze its advantages and disadvantages, use an incremental implementation process, and see how it can operate in the real world of schools, teachers, and students.

UNDERSTANDING THE NATURE OF SELF-DIRECTED DEVELOPMENT

Self-directed development is a supervisory option for highly qualified teachers who prefer to work on their own by becoming directly responsible for their own professional development. Other terms used to designate this option include the following: *self-supervision, individualized development,* and *independent supervision.* While the details will vary from school to school, most self-directed options include the following components.

- Guiding the teacher in setting learning-centered goals. The recommendation here is that teachers list only one goal that is related directly to learning. Some schools use two, three, or four goals and permit the teacher to list personal or professional goals. However, one learning goal focuses attention and reminds teachers of the central goal for all.

- Providing the needed resources for accomplishing those goals. Ordinarily, a small budget of $100 to $200 is sufficient.
- Working out together a plan for achieving those goals. A detailed plan will help the teacher work effectively and prove to the principal that the teacher is serious.
- Helping the teacher make interim and summative assessments. The teacher will need help in determining how to assess student progress.

ANALYZING THE ADVANTAGES AND DISADVANTAGES OF SELF-DIRECTED DEVELOPMENT

Like all of the supervisory options, self-directed development has its own advantages and disadvantages.

Its Advantages

Several advantages make it worth your consideration. First, it gives the teacher maximum flexibility in identifying developmental goals. Each teacher identifies the goals he or she wishes to achieve. There is no need to buy into group or faculty goals. Also, it can reduce the supervisory burden of supervisors and administrators. There is no need to make perfunctory observations of all teachers. Observations are undertaken only when they can contribute to the assessment process. Finally, it can develop in teachers the skills and attitudes necessary for continued professional growth.

Its Disadvantages

The chief drawback is that some teachers who have low standards for themselves may set easy-to-reach goals. Since the process relies on the teacher's ability to set and achieve goals, it is relatively easy for marginal teachers to manipulate the system so that their weaknesses go unperceived and unremedied. For this reason, it is recommended only for competent, experienced teachers. New teachers and marginal teachers need the more rigorous intensive development.

Also, many of the self-directed models do not build enough feedback into the way they operate. Feedback is essential for professional growth. The feedback can take several forms: report of observation of classroom by supervisor or administrator, test results, survey of student opinions, reflections by the teacher, and analysis of student portfolios.

In addition to these basic flaws, it can also overwhelm the participants with the burdens of coping with the paperwork and holding conferences. In developing the model, school leaders should keep these problems in mind.

USING IMPLEMENTATION STRATEGIES

Schools are encouraged to use an incremental implementation process since the model has a significant impact on all involved. The following steps are taken in many of the models.

1. A task force of teachers, supervisors, and administrators uses multiple sources of input to develop the general framework for each school's model. In developing the framework, the task force should review the experience of other schools, the general research on the model, and the constraints posed by the school system (see Glatthorn, 1997). The recommendation here is that the school district should develop general district guidelines but give each school considerable autonomy in developing school-based models. The school, in turn, should be sure that the school model draws upon the knowledge of the teachers since teacher acceptance is a vital element in the model's success.

2. Provide the needed staff development for the school administrators and supervisors who must implement the program. This staff development is essential since the models require new skills for all the participants. The following topics are typically presented.

Figure 8.1   Staff Development Topics for Teachers Using the Self-Directed Model

1. Understanding the self-directed model

2. Identifying learning-centered goals

3. Specifying actions for achieving goals

4. Identifying needed resources

5. Building in feedback

6. Assessing and reporting progress

Figure 8.2   Staff Development for Administrators and Supervisors Using the
Self-Directed Model

1. Orienting the faculty and informing parents

2. Helping teachers identify learning-centered goals

3. Helping teachers identify actions and resources for achieving goals

4. Helping teachers make formative evaluations

5. Monitoring the implementation and making formative evaluations

Figure 8.1 lists the topics that should be presented to administrators and supervisors; Figure 8.2 lists those presented to teachers.

3. Implement the school-based model on a pilot basis, monitoring as implementation progresses. The monitoring strategies can include the following: surveys of teachers, interviews and group discussions of supervisors and administrators, and evaluation of artifacts, such as the self-directed protocols described below.

4. Use the results of the monitoring to fine-tune the local model.

SEEING HOW IT MIGHT OPERATE AT THE SCHOOL LEVEL

The following discussion offers some specific recommendations so that you can gain a fuller understanding of the model.

First, the teacher should complete and submit the *self-development protocol*. Figure 8.3 shows an example of such a protocol. Certain features should be noted here. First, one goal is proposed, and that goal is directly related to student learning. Also, the teacher delineates the specific steps he or she plans to take to accomplish the goal. Next, the teacher indicates how progress will be assessed. To remind the teacher of the importance of feedback, the teacher is asked to specify the feedback sources. Finally, the teacher notes the resources he or she will need.

If the principal has a question about any of the items, a written comment or an informal conference can clarify the concerns.

Figure 8.3   Sample of Self-Directed Protocol

1. I will improve student learning by *improving my skills in teaching mathematical problem solving.*

2. I hope to accomplish this goal by taking the following actions:

   a. Review research on teaching problem solving

   b. Attend workshop in mathematical problem solving

   c. Develop two units in mathematical problem solving

   d. Teach two lessons from unit

   e. Ask department chair to observe sample lessons and evaluate the units

3. I will assess my progress by *administering a problem-solving test, with 70 percent of students achieving 70 percent mastery.*

4. I will solicit and use the following feedback:

   a. Observation of two lessons by department chair

   b. Evaluation of units by department chair and students

   c. Analysis of test results

5. I will need the following resources:

   a. $100 for workshop fee

   b. Additional planning time once every two weeks

Using Cooperative Development With Highly Qualified Teachers

As explained in Chapter 4, cooperative development uses a team or group structure to develop highly qualified teachers. This chapter presents a rationale for cooperative development, recommends a structure for this aspect of faculty growth, describes the activities that the team can undertake, and notes some cautions in using cooperative teams.

A RATIONALE FOR USING TEAMS FOR THE DEVELOPMENT OF TEACHERS

All schools use teams, even though they may not use "team teaching." They appear as grade-level groups in elementary schools and as subject-centered departments in high school. Middle schools vary. The argument here is that, for several reasons, such groups should be used as one of the primary mechanisms for the development of teachers.

The new teachers profit in several ways. They feel accepted and secure in a professional home where they can make a contribution. They develop their skills by being coached by colleagues who are available and trustworthy—not by a remote supervisor who drops in once in a while. They get their questions answered quickly in a natural environment. The team—and, in turn, the school—benefits from their contributions as they work as active members of problem-solving groups.

A STRUCTURE FOR COOPERATIVE DEVELOPMENT

Before making recommendations for organizing teams, it would be helpful to analyze the three models available to you.

Active Team, Less Active Mentor

In this model, the team is expected to play an active role in school improvement as well as helping the new teacher acquire the knowledge and skills. The mentor plays a somewhat inactive role, yielding to the needs of the team. The main drawback with this model is that the team alone has difficulty handling all the developmental responsibilities.

Less Active Team, Active Mentor

In this model, the team is a team in name only. Members of the team manifest the dangers of what Hargreaves and Dawe (1990) call "contrived collegiality," a situation in which principals attempt to mandate cooperation on a reluctant faculty of individuals. The mentor is the chief source of all teacher learning. The drawback here is that it puts too much responsibility on a busy mentor.

Active Team, Active Mentor

In this model, the team and the mentor cooperate actively in the twin tasks of improving the school and developing the new teacher. The new teacher is an active participant in the interactions of the team, learning in a somewhat informal way. As the new teacher exhibits the need for specific skill development, the mentor then takes over, working with the teacher individually. The "active team, active mentor" is the model recommended here, using the team structure that presently exists in your school. Typically, that would mean using grade-level teams for elementary schools and subject matter departments for high schools. Use subject matter teams in the middle school if the program is departmentalized; use grade-level middle school teams if the school's program and philosophy are student centered. The important point is not to create one more bureaucratic structure.

In that existing structure, the teachers play an active role. They work with colleagues in developing and implementing school improvement plans. They cooperatively develop curriculum units based on state curriculum standards. They collaborate in developing long-term instructional plans. They are acquiring job-related skills in their workplace environment.

If they need special help with one of the essential teaching skills, they then work individually with their mentor. If organizationally feasible, the mentor is part of the same instructional team. The main drawback to this model is that the teacher may be receiving too much help—often of a conflicting nature.

ACTIVITIES TO HELP IN THE DEVELOPMENT OF TEACHERS

The active team can play a key role in developing new teachers, serving as a more effective substitute for standard supervision (see Glatthorn, 1997). The following activities have been reported to be effective.

Action Research

In this model, the team uses a problem-solving approach to solve a learning-related problem. This syncretic model seems to work well (see Calhoun, 2002, for other approaches).

1. The team senses the existence of a concern—a vague deficiency that affects learning. The concern can be sensed from several data sources: teachers' observations, attendance data, parent conferences, student health reports, discipline reports, and test scores. Here are some concerns that teams have attacked:

   - Many students are ill.
   - Advanced math courses are dropping in enrollment.
   - We need more help in the classroom.

2. The team studies the concern, answering the questions of who, what, when, where, why, and how. The study at this time is to narrow the focus by turning the concern into a clearly defined problem. Here is an example.

   - CONCERN. Our students aren't motivated.
   - PROBLEM. Eighth-grade girls are not motivated to achieve in math.

3. Based on the study of the concern, the team identifies the problem. The problem should be clearly stated, sharply focused, and capable of being solved by the team.

4. The team engages in knowledge building, determining what the research and exemplary practice might contribute to solving the problem. The team can do a better job of solving the problem if it knows what has worked elsewhere.

5. The team draws on the knowledge base and its creativity in generating solutions to the problem.

6. The team evaluates the solutions to develop a solution set, a composite of the best ideas.

7. The team implements the solution set, monitoring how well it is working.

Working through that model might take two or three years. It is time-consuming but educative.

Critical Friends

The critical friends approach emphasizes the importance of collegial feedback. In this system, a small group of colleagues meets periodically to give each other feedback. They might critically review an assignment a colleague has developed or a unit that one member has written. In the "lesson study" approach (developed originally in Japan), the critical friends engage in a close analysis of a videotaped lesson that one of the group has taught (see Bambino, 2002; Watanabe, 2002). In some versions of this model, the lesson is retaught and retaped after the analysis.

A variation of this approach focuses on group analysis of student strengths and needs and the methods by which those needs might be met. *Whole Faculty Study Groups*, by Murphy and Lick (2001), explains in detail how this model has worked successfully in several schools.

Peer Supervision

In this model, the group functions as a supervisor of a colleague, working through an approach to clinical supervision. Most peer groups use a rather simple model of clinical supervision: hold a lesson plan discussion, observe the colleague, and hold a feedback conference. The main problem with this model is that colleagues find it very difficult to give constructive criticism to one another. When observing a peer supervisor at work, one hears only "happy talk" about the strengths of a lesson (see Glatthorn, 1997).

Despite this problem, peer supervision can be effective in helping a marginal teacher improve. If the team can provide both support and constructive feedback, the marginal teacher can make great strides (see Chapter 7).

Professional Dialogs

This model provides a simple structure for teachers to discuss educational issues. A professional book or article is selected—one that deals with a current issue or a new approach. After reading the resource, teachers discuss these questions:

1. "What say?" What are the essential ideas?

2. "How good?" What is the quality of the argument? Is it well supported by sound reasoning and good research?

3. "So what?" What shall we do—take action, study the issue, or move on?

A useful set of guidelines for effective dialogs is provided by Routman (2002).

Curriculum Units

The development of standards-based curriculum units is an educative process that results in a product teachers can use. Several models are available, including the one presented in Chapter 11 and described more fully in Glatthorn (1999).

1. Develop a scope and sequence chart by identifying the curriculum standards and their benchmarks for particular subjects. The standards are statements of what students are to learn by the end of Grade 12. The benchmarks spell out the grade-level expectations for the standards.

2. Organize the benchmarks into unit titles. The unit title is used to identify the general goal of the unit.

3. Develop a semester or year calendar showing the sequence of unit titles. This long-term calendar, which shows how long each unit takes, helps the team plan its teaching so that the curriculum is adequately covered.

4. For each unit title, identify the performance tasks and their rubrics. The performance task is a complex problem that the students are to solve to demonstrate their learning. The rubrics explain to the teacher how to assess student performance.

CAUTIONS TO KEEP IN MIND IN USING TEAMS

Despite the fact that these approaches are reported to be effective, there are certain cautions to keep in mind.

First, they all require special training of the teacher participants, who will have to learn a new set of skills and knowledge. Each approach has its own demands. Here, for example, are some of the skills involved in the lesson study.

- Seeing the whole lesson
- Assessing the learning involved
- Identifying the learning obstacles and facilitators
- Helping the teacher see and accept

Next, they all take considerable time, and time is always in short supply. Schools that have successfully used these approaches report that they provided released time for teachers to work together.

Note also that several approaches expect teachers to give each other feedback, at times of a critical sort. Teachers espouse a norm of equality— "We are all good teachers." They are thus reluctant to give any constructive feedback, even when couched in professional terms.

Finally, all these strategies will work effectively only if they are employed in a school that genuinely values collegiality.

Working With Mentors to Develop Highly Qualified Teachers

This chapter begins by providing some background information about the nature of mentoring. It then explains how to make your mentoring program more effective.

UNDERSTANDING THE NATURE OF MENTORING

For centuries, mentors have functioned as guides and role models for their protégés. In so doing, they often seem to reenact the original story of how the departing Odysseus asked Mentor to watch over Telemachus, the son of Odysseus. Almost all of these mentor-protégé relationships have developed informally. For example, an aspiring architect might begin an apprenticeship with a master architect. They find that they can work together well. Much of the protégé's learning comes about informally, as he or she works at the side of the master. While they work together, the protégé finds that the master architect is performing several critical functions: modeling, demonstrating, coaching, giving constructive feedback, and shaping the professional values. As they work together, they may not use the term *mentor.* Years later, the one who was mentored will probably look back and say, "She was my mentor."

Now educators concerned with the development of new teachers have taken the term with most of its distinguishing features, applying them to a formally assigned master teacher who is expected to guide the new teacher safely through the shoals of the initial years of teaching. This teacher mentor is often selected by the principal to work with a novice teacher; thus, in education, the mentor-protégé relationship is more formal and carefully structured than in the original sense. And it may well happen that a novice has both a formally designated mentor and an unofficial one whom the novice seeks out. It should be noted here that in some educational circles, the neologism *mentee* is used to designate the person here referred to as the *protégé*.

The teacher mentor is usually rewarded in several ways. He or she is given released time since the role demands a great deal of extra time. Many districts pay the mentor a stipend for the extra services rendered. And many mentors testify that their greatest reward is their own professional growth as they work collaboratively with the protégé (see Podsen & Denmark, 2000).

Mentoring programs can be expensive. One study of California's new teacher mentoring program concluded that program costs totaled $5,000 per teacher—but concluded that the program was well worth the expense (California Commission on Teacher Credentialing, 1992). Other studies have also affirmed the effectiveness of such programs (see Arends & Rigazio-DiGilio, 2000).

Carving out a special role for the mentor in no way depreciates the importance of other helpers. In one study, elementary teachers reported that their principal was of more help than the mentor; secondary teachers perceived other colleagues more effective than their mentors (Marso & Pigge, 1990).

SELECTING MENTORS

Selecting an effective mentor for a teacher is a complicated process. Some principals find it so complicated that they defer making the choice. They do so by assigning a "buddy" for the first few weeks who is responsible for helping the new teacher get off to a smooth start. The buddy is a highly accessible information source for answers to questions about taking attendance, handling major discipline problems, assigning homework, and passing out textbooks. Both the buddy and the new teacher understand that the arrangement is only temporary. This temporary buddy system buys some time for assigning the mentor while ensuring that the teacher survives the first few weeks in good shape.

Regardless of when the permanent mentor is assigned, there is still a need to choose mentors who meet the following criteria.

- Are known to be highly effective teachers, able to model the skills they hope to impart to the protégé
- Are perceived by other teachers as moral leaders with a strong commitment to the profession
- Understand the nature of teachers' professional development and are able to apply that knowledge in working with the protégé
- Understand the nature of the culture of both the school and the community
- Know the unwritten norms of behavior to which the new teacher should conform (e.g., is there an unwritten dress code for teachers?)
- Have a high degree of interpersonal sensitivity, knowing how to listen and how to respond, when to intervene and when to let the protégé solve the problem

In addition to these general traits, some specific similarities and differences seem to facilitate the relationship. Most school leaders feel that the mentor and the protégé should be the same gender, to minimize relationship problems. Teachers from alternative programs should be matched with mentors who are not biased against them because of the nature of their preparation. Finally, the nature of mentoring suggests that the mentor should be at least a few years older than the protégé. Note, however, that some experienced principals do not find this matching process helpful.

TRAINING MENTORS

Mentors will need to be trained, either as a group or individually. The training should be organized and delivered in a manner that reflects the best research and experience. The following features should characterize training programs.[1]

- The training is individualized, based on assessments of individual needs.
- The training is provided at a time convenient to mentors, when they feel fresh and positive.
- The training provides a sound knowledge base for the essential skills.
- The skills that make up the training agenda are derived from an analysis of the mentor's role.
- The training gets the mentors involved as active participants and contributors.
- The training makes effective use of the technology.

- The training is systematic, ongoing, and continuous, not a collection of "one-shot" programs.
- The training provided at the school site is coordinated with whatever graduate course work is concurrently taken.

As noted above, the content of the training should respond to the specific needs of the mentor. The agenda suggested in Figure 10.1 shows one typical set of training sessions.

Figure 10.1   Content of Typical Mentor Training Programs

1. Understanding the relationship of mentoring to student learning

2. Carrying out the mentor role

3. Communicating effectively as a mentor

4. Helping the novice teacher understand the culture of this school

5. Diagnosing the needs of the novice teacher

6. Providing a knowledge base for skill development

7. Understanding and developing the essential skills of teaching

8. Providing emotional support as needed

IDENTIFYING MENTOR FUNCTIONS

The work of the mentor can best be understood in the context of a comprehensive approach that integrates the work of the mentor with that of other professionals. All the professionals involved in the development of new teachers can perform their tasks more effectively if they have a clear understanding of their responsibilities. A process for aligning responsibilities is highlighted in Figure 10.2. Each function is discussed below, with a recommendation based on research and experience. However, you should make your own decisions here, based on your school's needs and resources. The form shown in Figure 10.2 can facilitate your own decision making.

1. Provide emotional support. This function will vary in its need, based on the emotional intelligence of the new teacher. It involves several essential responses: giving earned praise, accepting feelings, providing emotional distance as needed, listening and responding empathically, and helping the teacher handle emotional crises. The mentor should be primarily responsible, with the team assisting.

Figure 10.2   Professional Development Functions

Directions: Listed below are the functions required in the professional development of new teachers. Across the top of the chart are those who might perform them. For each function, indicate who is primarily RESPONSIBLE by putting an R in the appropriate cell. Use only one R for each function. Then indicate who may ASSIST with that function by putting an A in the appropriate cell. You may use more than one A for each function.

Function	Principal, Assistant	Central Office	Mentor	Teaching Team	Counselor
1. Provide emotional support					
2. Provide information about school					
3. Provide information about community					
4. Provide information about students					
5. Provide materials for teaching					
6. Coach for skill development, making developmental observations					
7. Help teacher understand culture					
8. Conduct formal evaluations					
9. Provide a teachable assignment					
10. Make informal observations					

2. Provide information about the school. Much of this information should be in print or available electronically. The principal or assistant principal should be primarily responsible, assisted by the mentor and the team.

3. Provide information about the community. The new teacher most of all needs to know the unwritten norms that the community expects the teachers to respect. The mentor can perhaps best perform this function, assisted by someone from the central office.

4. Provide information about students. The new teacher is not especially concerned about students in general but about his or her students in particular. A guidance counselor assisted by the team can help here. It should be noted, however, that many experienced teachers do not study their students' cumulative folders at the start of the school year. They prefer to let each student start fresh. One teacher put it this way: "I don't care how Johnny did last year for Ms. Morgan—I just care about how he does this year for me."

5. Provide materials for teaching. The mentor should be primarily responsible for helping the teacher find and make appropriate teaching materials. The team can assist in helping here, emphasizing the effective use of the text.

6. Coach for skill development, making developmental observations. The mentor should lead here, doing what is usually termed *supervision*. The team can assist here, using the "lesson study" approach previously explained.

7. Help the new teacher understand the culture of the school. The culture includes the following: the operating values of the school, the norms of behavior ("this is how we do things around here"), the heroes, the stories, and the celebrations. Probably the mentor assisted by the teaching team can best understand and impart the culture.

8. Conduct formal evaluations. The principal or the assistant principal should carry out this function. Mentors should not evaluate. The mentor-protégé relationship should emphasize teacher development, provided in an atmosphere of openness and trust. Evaluation is an essential administrative function, but it results in closing the communication channels. If the local context requires

the mentor to evaluate, then the mentor should be sure to stress the difference: "My next observation and conference will be evaluative—let me explain what that means."

9. Provide a teachable assignment. These are the hallmarks of a teachable assignment: teaches in field, has no more than three preparations, has adequate time for planning, is assigned manageable classes, teaches in no more than two different locations, and has reasonable class size.

10. Make informal observations. An informal observation is one that lasts from five to ten minutes. These observations keep the observer visible, demonstrate a classroom orientation, provide an opportunity for earned praise, alert the observer to the developing problem, and assist in monitoring the curriculum.

SOLVING MENTOR PROBLEMS

Even the best mentor programs can encounter problems. The general advice is to work with the mentor and the teacher to help them develop win-win solutions to the four most common problems. A general strategy is offered for each problem.

1. *The teacher asks for a new mentor.* After listening to the complaint, the principal should encourage the teacher to work out the difficulty with the mentor. If that does not work, the principal should meet with them both. As a last resort, the principal may need to make the change.

2. *The mentor is spending too much time in tasks not related to the mentor role.* The research notes this as a very common problem. The mentor gets caught up in such projects as developing curricula, chairing committees, and taking care of paperwork. The principal needs to work with the mentor in a problem-solving mode to identify the causes and find a solution.

3. *The mentor complains that the mentoring role is taking so much time that his or her own classes are being neglected.* Since mentors tend to be master teachers who care about their own students, they will often find themselves in this role conflict. The principal needs to do some empathic listening before moving to a problem-solving mode. Priorities need to be set and time management strategies employed.

4. *The rest of the faculty complain about the mentoring program.* Complaints are predictable since mentoring flies in the face of the faculty value of egalitarianism—"we are all master teachers." The principal needs to provide proactive leadership here, stressing the benefits to the school of the mentoring program.

NOTE

1. The following sources were used: Fullan (1995), Little (1990), and Sparks and Hirsh (1997).

Using Curriculum Development as Faculty Development

This chapter argues that curriculum development can be an effective tool for faculty development. The chapter begins by presenting the rationale for this position and then explains in step-by-step fashion a process for curriculum development.

A RATIONALE FOR CURRICULUM DEVELOPMENT AS FACULTY DEVELOPMENT

Developing effective curricula is an essential component of school improvement (see, e.g., Cotton, 1995). If the process involves the entire faculty, then it can have several benefits for faculty growth. First, it enables the faculty to become familiar with state and school system curriculum documents. Almost all states have now developed and implemented curriculum standards that specify what students are to learn, grade by grade and subject by subject. These standards then become the basis of the state tests that are then used for several purposes—evaluating student learning, assessing school effectiveness, and judging teacher quality. Using state standards helps teachers understand these documents in detail.

There are other benefits to using curriculum work as a catalyst for professional growth. Teachers usually enjoy the chance to work with colleagues in a productive enterprise. In this manner, they also learn from colleagues about the nature of curriculum change. And the work results in materials that facilitate teacher planning.

USING CURRICULUM STANDARDS

Curriculum standards are so widely used in curriculum work that they have become an intrinsic component of curriculum development. Curriculum standards are statements of what students should be learning in each grade, for each subject. For example, here is a science standard for Grades 3 to 5:

> Knows the major differences between fresh and ocean waters (Marzano & Kendall, 1999, p. 177)

Almost every state has adopted curriculum standards for every subject and has published curriculum materials to support them. As a result, most school districts in that state have used the standards to develop curriculum guides. And every subject matter organization has published its own standards for the subject that concerns it.

Not everyone is happy about state and district standards. Some criticize the top-down process by which they were developed. Others worry that they will reduce teachers' creativity since teachers no longer decide what to teach. Finally, many are convinced that the standards are unrealistic, especially for disadvantaged students.

They do seem to have some value. They have been drawn from the best professional advice. They constitute a quality curriculum for all students. They eliminate the curricular anarchy resulting from a "do your own thing" approach.

DEVELOPING POSITIVE FACULTY ATTITUDES

A special workshop should be held for all new teachers since many teacher education programs do not help preservice teachers use curriculum standards in implementing curriculum. The first step is to develop with all teachers a positive attitude toward curriculum standards. While teachers in general accept standards as a fact of school life, some are still reluctant to embrace them (see Glatthorn & Fontana, 2000). Some principals have found that teachers from alternative teacher preparation programs seem less likely to resist standards. Such teachers have come from a work environment characterized by standardization and top-down decision making. The message to all teachers is the following:

> Standards are here, along with state tests based on them. Let's make the best use of the standards and the tests.

DEVELOPING A SCOPE AND SEQUENCE CHART

The standards can be used in the next step in the process—developing a scope and sequence chart. A scope and sequence chart lists for one subject all the essential learnings or benchmarks for each grade. Benchmarks are the grade-level outcomes for each standard. For example, here is a benchmark for the standard noted earlier: identifies components of ocean waters.

If the school system has not previously developed its own scope and sequence chart, then teams of teachers should work together to do so. The process is a simple one. Grade-level or departmental teams should review the state and professional standards for their grade level or department. (A good source for professional standards is Marzano & Kendall, 1999.) They should also examine textbooks in their field. Finally, they should reflect about their knowledge of the state tests, using only publicly available state documents.

Each team would then indicate in the appropriate cell the benchmarks for their grade level, for each strand or division of the subject. Then, a school-wide committee should review all the entries on the scope and sequence chart, asking the following questions:

- Is the placement of benchmarks developmentally appropriate?
- Does the allocation of benchmarks to given grade levels result in balanced loads so that the teachers in one grade level or subject do not have an excessive number of benchmarks to teach?
- Does the progression within each strand show reinforcement and development, without excessive repetition?
- Do all benchmarks adequately reflect the state standards?

The answers to these questions should help them determine which revisions are needed. That revised scope and sequence chart can then be used by teams to develop long-term plans and units of study.

In the approach used here, the long-term plan is the master plan for organizing units and allocating time to each unit. The unit plans are derived from the long-term plan, and the daily plans come from the unit plan. Thus, lessons have coherence with each other, rather than seeming like fragmented and isolated entities.

DEVELOPING LONG-TERM PLANS

Teachers should develop for their own benefit a long-term plan for each course they teach that lasts for the entire school year. Semester plans should be developed for courses meeting for only one term. (In the following discussion, the modifier *long-term* is used to identify both yearly and semester plans.) Long-term plans are important to teachers for several reasons. They help teachers pace learning over a long period of time, ensuring that all the major objectives are accomplished. They remind teachers which units they will be teaching, when they will be taught, and in which sequence. Such reminders make it easier for teachers to schedule special resources, such as speakers and films. They indicate the time to be allotted to each unit—a critical component in student achievement. And they relate unit planning to key events that will probably influence planning, such as the administration of standardized tests. Although ignored by many school administrators and teachers, long-term plans are a key component of the classroom curriculum. There are many methods teachers can use in developing long-term plans. The process explained below has worked well for many teachers.

PAINTING A PORTRAIT OF THE YEAR

The next step in the process is to paint a portrait of the year—the big picture that enables teachers to think globally before thinking particularly. By considering the general goals for the subject taught (usually by reviewing the curriculum guide and the scope and sequence chart) and the developmental level of their students, teachers reflect about what they really want for the students from that year's work. Teachers should also check the curriculum guide's grade-level objectives or benchmarks for that subject, examine the texts (and other learning materials) and tests (both end-of-course and standardized tests), and reflect about the students, their needs, their interests, and their community. Finally, they bring to bear their own knowledge of teaching and their own values with respect to that subject. The results of all that data gathering and reflection are then summarized in a portrait of the year's work.

Here is an example of the portrait that a team of eighth-grade teachers produced as they planned a science course.

Our students need to see that science is exciting—that it touches them all. So we could start with their own rural community. Maybe do some practical work on conservation, emphasizing what they and their families can do. Maybe we could do an integrated unit with social studies and language arts. We could teach a practical unit on letter writing—how to influence local governments. And since we are not far from the ocean, we could do a unit on oceans, maybe taking an extended field trip. About that time we should have a unit on matter. And the changes in matter. That would be a good time for another exciting unit, on science and their bodies. We should check with the health ed teachers to cooperate here, not compete for territory. We could then have them study machines, from a scientific point of view. Maybe by that time they would be ready for a unit on the plant kingdom, again relating it to our community. We could then follow up with a brief unit on fungi, algae, bacteria, and viruses, again emphasizing the personal health aspects. (Adapted from Glatthorn & Sheerer, 2004)

From that very general and somewhat subjective portrait, teachers then move to the next steps in the process.

IDENTIFYING THE TITLES OF UNITS

The next step is to identify the titles of the units. The term *unit* is used here to mean a series of organized lessons all related to some general concept, theme, or skill. Identifying the title should help teachers determine the main focus of the units that teachers will teach. Several steps are involved here.

Review the portrait to see the big picture. As shown in the example above, it will often make reference to unit themes. Then determine the organizing principle or principles to be used in developing units. Here are some options to consider: general concepts ("Ecology"), major themes ("Families First"), complex skills ("Writing Persuasively"), and time periods ("The Thirties"). Also decide the approximate number of units teachers will be able to teach effectively, considering the nature of the learners and the need for depth of understanding. Teachers should also review briefly the learning materials available and the tests their students must take; the former will suggest unit titles; the latter, the constraints that will operate. Upon the basis of all these analyses, the teachers should then make a tentative decision about unit titles, reviewing them to check whether they are likely to achieve the subject goals.

The planning team should also determine the sequence of the units, being sensitive to seasonal interests of their students and their awareness of national holidays, especially for younger students. They should also consider the relationship of the units to each other and the principles of learning.

ALLOCATING TIME TO EACH UNIT

Time allocations are important since time and learning are so closely related. The time can perhaps best be represented by the number of instructional periods to be devoted to the unit; an instructional period is defined as a clearly demarcated session lasting from thirty to eighty minutes. The planning team should make this decision by determining the relative importance and complexity of each unit and allocating periods to each unit, ensuring sufficient time for depth of learning and problem solving.

RECORDING DECISIONS IN A LONG-TERM CALENDAR

The team should next record all the major decisions in a long-term calendar. The calendar should list the weeks of the school year, the major events occurring throughout the year, and the title of each unit. The "major events" column is important; it serves as a reminder of school and community activities that would impinge on teaching and learning. The column would note such events as the following: national and state holidays, vacation periods, major testing dates, parent meetings, and major social events (such as the senior prom). Teachers may also decide to include on the calendar other information, such as the type of unit (whether integrated or subject focused), the major objectives or benchmarks taught in the unit, the resources needed, and the total number of periods allocated to the unit. Whatever information teachers consider important in long-term planning should be included.

The format of the calendar is not important. An example of the format suggested above, which works well for one subject, is shown in Figure 11.1. Many elementary teachers use a different format. The subjects

Figure 11.1 Long-Term Plan

Dates	Major Events	Unit Title	Unit Type	Benchmarks or Objectives	Resources
9/4–9/8	Yom Kippur	Keeping a journal	Not integrated	Use journal as a record of major events	Amiel's journal
9/11–9/15		Semiotics: Reading the signs	Integrated English	Interpret signs of the local culture	*The Signs of Our Times*, Solomon
9/18–9/22	Parents Night	See above			

they teach are listed down the left side of the chart. Across the top are the weeks of the school year. They enter in the appropriate cell the titles of the units they plan to teach.

WRITING UNITS OF STUDY

One of the most important aspects of teachers' curriculum work is the development of units of study. Unit planning is much more significant in the learning process than daily planning since the unit level is best for providing for curriculum integration and for showing plans to emphasize problem solving. The following discussion explains one process for developing units that emphasize critical thinking and problem solving. The teachers should begin by selecting a unit title from the list developed for the long-term calendar, then proceed in step-by-step fashion as follows.

(Several models of unit development are available; the following has worked well in faculty staff development workshops.)

Block in the Unit

The first step is to *block in the unit.* The blocking process establishes the general limits within which teachers will work. Teachers make several decisions—or confirm some decisions previously made: the title of the unit, the length of the unit, the unit goal, and the problem to be solved. After tentatively identifying the problem to be solved, teachers should next reflect about the unit goal previously stated, considering several factors: the time available, the students' knowledge and interests, and the materials available. This reflection process may suggest the need to reframe the unit goal—to modify its general thrust or to make the goal more sharply focused. The next step is one not ordinarily found in curriculum texts, but it is one that has been especially effective in working with classroom teachers. The *unit scenario* is a script for the unit, similar to the portrait of the year. It explains in general form how the unit begins, how it moves through the stages of learning, and how it ends. It includes some reference to the major ways the students will learn. In brief, before teachers get into the details of the lesson objectives and activities, they delineate the big picture.

Teachers develop the scenario by first reflecting, imagining, and brainstorming in a somewhat freewheeling manner. As ideas crystallize, the planners jot them down, continuing in this manner until they have a very clear mental picture of the major components and flow of the unit. The final step is to write a clear draft that can guide teachers and their colleagues. Here is the first draft of the unit scenario for the unit on family change.

Start the unit by having students interview their grandparents, finding out what families were like when the grandparents were children. They will have to be taught some interviewing skills. If major cultural differences develop, we will cast them in a positive light. We should then have them investigate the factors that influence family change. We will need to find some materials on the topic that they can handle. Then they can work in groups to predict further family change, say, twenty years from now. They could demonstrate their learning by having the students produce a couple dramatizations.

When teachers have finished the first draft of the scenario, they should check it against the criteria for unit excellence identified below. This is only a preliminary check, to ensure that the unit is moving in the right direction.

Developing the unit scenario is a very useful mental process to assist teachers in planning. In many ways, the mental processes are more important than the writing. And the unit scenario helps teachers do the mental planning. However, teachers do not have to record the scenario in the unit itself.

Determining Knowledge Needed and Means of Access

With the scenario in mind, teachers then reflect about the knowledge needed and how students will gain access to that knowledge. Students can best solve problems when they have in-depth knowledge relative to the problem. In this sense, this unit model synthesizes content and process, rather than seeing them as separate entities. Learners acquire knowledge— and then make that knowledge generative in solving the problem.

Determine Which Learning
Strategies Students Will Need to Learn

Learning strategies are the mental operations that help in the problem-solving process. Some are generic, used in several subjects, such as using web diagrams to suggest connections; some are subject specific, such as listing all the known elements in solving mathematical problems. Such strategies are better taught in context, not in isolation.

Sketch In the Lesson Plans

With the unit-level planning completed, teachers now move to the lesson level. But lessons are not developed out of thin air but derive from all the work done thus far at the unit planning level. Thus, a lesson is derived from the unit; a unit is not a random collection of lessons. Several lesson-planning models are available. One that teachers can use is presented in the next section.

Evaluate and Disseminate the Unit

The unit should be carefully evaluated before it is disseminated. To guide the process of unit evaluation, apply the following criteria.

- The unit is outcome focused: The unit goal or key outcome is clearly stated, and the lesson objectives or outcomes are directly related to the unit goal.
- The unit makes appropriate integration of content from that subject (or from two or more subjects), as well as making use of writing and reading as ways of learning.
- The unit emphasizes depth, not superficiality, with sufficient time provided to achieve depth of understanding.
- The unit focuses on problem solving and critical thinking, in the context of real situations.
- The unit has appropriate sequence and coherence, so that lessons build on and relate to each other.
- The unit emphasizes active learning, one that sees the learner as an active maker of meaning and a cognitive apprentice, using generative knowledge to solve meaningful problems.
- The unit emphasizes a social context for learning, with effective use of cooperative learning and student interaction.
- The learning activities recommended are directly related to the outcomes, are likely to achieve the outcomes, and are developmentally appropriate.
- The unit makes appropriate provisions for individual differences and is especially sensitive to the needs and strengths of students from minority ethnic groups.
- The unit provides for authentic assessment of student learning.

The final step is to prepare the unit for peer review and dissemination. The teachers should systematize all the previous decisions, add the necessary details, and prepare a review draft for colleagues to evaluate the unit.

Regardless of how the lesson is derived or which format is used, teachers and supervisors should keep in mind these tested principles of good lesson design—remembering that they are only general guidelines, not iron-clad rules.

Good lessons enable learners

1. to make connections with what has gone before, to get the big picture of what is to come, and to find a reason and motivation to learn;

2. to understand what the lesson's objectives are;

3. to activate prior knowledge;

4. to get efficient access to new knowledge;

5. to learn actively, using knowledge to solve problems;

6. to monitor their learning and make the needed adjustments;

7. to use metacognitive processes throughout, reflecting about their learning processes and their habits of thinking.

A FINAL NOTE

Developing all these materials is a complex and time-consuming task. However, the results are worth the effort. If carried out with due deliberation, they should produce some very useful documents and significant faculty growth.

PART IV

The Results

Retaining Highly Qualified Teachers

No matter how good your school system is in recruiting and selecting teachers, your approach is not effective if they leave after a few years of service. This chapter explores why the problem of teacher retention is important, why teachers leave, and what you can do to retain them.

UNDERSTANDING THE IMPORTANCE OF RETENTION

Consider these statistics. About 30 percent of new teachers leave within five years—regardless of the nature of their preparation program. And the rate is even higher in disadvantaged schools (Fox & Certo, 1999). Besides the nuisance of replacing new teachers, the problem is an expensive one. By analyzing their data, scholars studying the cost of these departures in Texas determined that the total cost was $2 billion each year (Southeast Center for Teaching Quality, 2001). They also determined that a good induction program that would reduce those figures markedly would cost only $500 to $800 for each inductee.

Do teachers from alternative preparation programs leave the profession in greater numbers than those from standard programs? The research is inconclusive. Some studies conclude that those from alternative programs are more inclined to leave. For example, Natriello and Zumwalt (1992) found that about 80 to 90 percent of mathematics teachers from standard programs remained in the profession, compared with 60 percent from alternative programs. On the other hand, an evaluation of the Pathways program determined that 81 percent of its graduates had remained in teaching for at least three years, compared with the national average of 71 percent (Clewell & Villegas, 2001).

Two cautions should be noted here about overemphasizing retention. First, some teachers should not be retained: Your school would be better off if the incompetent, the unmotivated, and the biased teachers are encouraged to leave. Second, retaining all the competent teachers does not ensure success. You still need effective leadership, strong parent support, and a coordinated curriculum, among other elements.

ANALYZING THE REASONS TEACHERS LEAVE THEIR POSITIONS

Some of their reasons for leaving are obvious and beyond your control, such as relocating to another area, securing a higher salary in another school system or in a different career, finding that the demands of family responsibilities and teaching are too onerous, developing health problems, and discovering that their teacher preparation program had not prepared them for the realities of teaching (see McCreight, 2000).

However, many of the causes cited by teachers for their leaving the profession are within your sphere of influence. According to several studies, the following professionally related causes have been reported (see Collins, 1999; Houston, Marshall, & McDavid, 1993; McCreight, 2000; Southeast Center for Teaching Quality, 2001).

Student and Classroom Problems

Teachers often cite two problems that have their genesis in the classroom. They are often given demanding assignments—large classes, full schedules, difficult students, brief preparation periods, and a mismatch between what teachers know and what they are required to teach. Many teachers also complain that poor student discipline has driven them from the profession. For them, every day is a struggle for control—a struggle that students usually win.

Problems With Lack of Support

Teachers who leave the profession cite three areas where they experienced a lack of support—from colleagues, from the principal, and from parents and the community. In many schools, the "old hands" believe in the "sink or swim" philosophy for all new teachers. One veteran teacher said, "I didn't get any support from the principal in disciplining kids—why should the new guy?" In schools with a tight clique structure, the new teacher feels shut out.

In low-achieving schools, teachers often perceive their principals as hands-off, uninvolved leaders. Like all novice professionals, they want active support from the leader. That support translates into such behaviors as giving well-deserved praise, following through on discipline referrals, ensuring that texts and supplies are available for all students, and siding with the teacher in a teacher-student conflict.

Finally, new teachers want to be appreciated by parents and the larger community. The constant stream of "teacher bashing" demoralizes teachers. With some justification, they feel they are being singled out as solely responsible for poor student achievement, when a fairer analysis holds parents and the community accountable for school success. (For the special problems in rural communities, see Collins, 1999.)

Professional Issues

Three of the problems causing teachers to leave can be classified as professional issues. Creative teachers who want to build their own curriculum and give their own tests decry the lack of autonomy inherent in state-produced curricula and tests. Many teachers who are place-bound to a small community know that there is little room for advancement. One teacher put the problem this way: "My wife is a local attorney with a solid practice. I have been teaching fifth grade for twenty years. We have a young principal who just got appointed. I think I might change careers. There is no future in teaching here for me." And most teachers report very negative feelings about the quality of the inservice with which they are provided. They complain about so-called experts who present dull lectures on the latest fad.

USING GENERAL PROCESSES FOR RETENTION

How do you prevent and deal with problems in a way that encourages highly qualified teachers to stay? The first part of this section suggests a general process for increasing their retention in your school and the profession.

Begin With an Assessment

To gain an indication of potential problems, you should have the teachers do a self-assessment. Begin by explaining the nature and use of the self-assessment shown in Figure 12.1. Assure all first-year teachers that the instrument has only a diagnostic purpose. The results will not be used in evaluating them. Administer the survey in late September, after the respondents have had an opportunity to begin working with students, colleagues, and the principal.

The process of scoring each return is simple. Assign numerical values to each type of response: A = 4 points, B = 3 points, C = 2 points, and D = 1 point. Administer the survey to all first-year teachers. Score each survey by adding the total number of points and dividing by eleven. The result is the mean score for each teacher.

Use the same process to compute the mean for each question. Now you can use the results to assess your school's power of retention and to identify specific weaknesses. Use the overall results to determine how your school rates in the retention game. Use the individual returns to suggest which specific problems need attention for that teacher. Then administer and score the survey again in late May, to see what differences developed between September and May.

In using such instruments, keep in mind that teachers are often reluctant to express candid views about why they are leaving, even when they are assured of confidentiality.

Provide a Teachable Assignment

A teachable assignment will make success attainable. Here are the key features.

- *Reasonable class size.* Large classes are more difficult to handle. A smaller class reduces the challenge of large groups.
- *Classes in the teacher's field.* An experienced teacher knows how to teach in a way that covers up his or her lack of depth. A novice makes the weakness blatantly obvious. Do not ask a new teacher with an English major to teach math. Subject knowledge matters.
- *Adequate preparation time.* The new teacher may need extra preparation time, for preparing long-term and daily plans, for writing curriculum units, and for working with a mentor.

Strengthen Community Ties

A teacher who has ties to the community is more likely to stay. Without manipulating beginners, make them aware of the opportunities for community involvement and encourage them to plant roots. Emphasize as well their need to understand the community and use it as a resource for learning.

Figure 12.1   Succeeding at and Staying a Teacher

Directions

Listed below are the factors that are linked to teacher success and retention. Consider each one as it applies to you and circle one of these responses.

A: This factor is strongly present in my case.

B: This factor is somewhat present in my case.

C: This factor is present only in a few instances.

D: This factor is not present in my case.

1. I have what I consider to be a teachable assignment.	A	B	C	D
2. My students in general are well behaved.	A	B	C	D
3. My colleagues accept and help me.	A	B	C	D
4. My principal supports me.	A	B	C	D
5. Parents and the community feel positive about me.	A	B	C	D
6. I have sufficient autonomy to succeed as a teacher.	A	B	C	D
7. I have a chance to be promoted in this system.	A	B	C	D
8. I participate in helpful inservice programs.	A	B	C	D
9. I know I will succeed as a teacher.	A	B	C	D
10. I have a mentor who helps me.	A	B	C	D
11. I am part of a cohesive community.	A	B	C	D

Focus on Discipline

Both the group meetings and the individual supervision should be designed and implemented in a manner that focuses on effective classroom management. Provide the teachers with quality materials on how to build strong learning communities.

USING SPECIFIC STRATEGIES

The teachers need support from three main sources: the principal, the mentor, and the team or department leader. However, the mentor should coordinate the activities, to ensure that the teacher is not overwhelmed with conflicting advice and observations.

The discussion that follows suggests how those three sources can provide effective support throughout the school year.

Support From the Principal

The principal, as the designated leader of the school, needs to play an active role in making the teacher's first year a successful one. Principals or assistant principals must provide specific support to these teachers. The administrator is key to the success of the new teacher because he or she sets the expectations for the work environment. Specific support needs to be given in the following ways and at the appropriate times:

• *Soon after the hiring process.* At this time, administrators can orient the teacher to the building and to the typical day of a teacher. Discussing duty times, the workday timetable, required paperwork, and other expectations of teachers (such as membership in the parent association) will help the teacher. It is also important to discuss the responsibilities of a teacher, including keeping accurate records, staying in the classroom (not leaving children alone without a responsible adult), and following procedures for emergency drills. In short, the administrator cannot assume that the teacher understands the multiple roles that a teacher plays throughout one school day.

• *At the beginning of the year.* If the teacher is hired at the beginning of the year, then the preliminary orientation will be a great help to him or her. Many times, teachers do not understand the need to use workdays effectively or the importance of setting up their classrooms early because of all the required meetings at the beginning of the year. Meeting with teachers at this point to orient them toward a successful beginning of the year will be crucial to their retention. At this time, the following areas need to be discussed:

Record Keeping

Be sure to orient these teachers to the need to keep accurate records of grades, test scores, and attendance.

Classroom Management Policies and Procedures

This is the most important area in retaining these teachers. It will be important to discuss the importance of having clear rules and consequences along with routines. Having models and handouts will be helpful with this component. Make it clear to these teachers which types of discipline offenses should be handled by the teacher and which types should be referred to administrators. Encourage the use of a discipline log so these teachers can track their own problems in the classroom. Having them read the teacher's handbook will be helpful. Stressing the need for partnerships with parents at all levels of school and the need not to counsel children and their parents about areas out of their control will help these teachers understand their role as a teacher.

Curriculum Development and Implementation

The third area to discuss at this point in the year is the development of effective lesson plans using a variety of strategies. While the mentor will be more helpful in this area on a day-to-day implementation of curriculum, the administrator can set the tone and provide general guidelines for curriculum work.

• *During the second and third weeks.* These early weeks are an overwhelming time for new teachers. Many times, it has been years since they have been in a school setting as a student, not in charge. Meeting with them as a small group to debrief about the week and answer questions about procedures, processes, and other schoolwide issues will make them feel supported. While experienced teachers do not depend on their principals for continued support because they are confident, new teachers depend on their principals for emotional support during their initial years of teaching.

• *The first month.* During the first month, the principal should make brief informal observations. These should be followed by more formal evaluative observations.

The Mentor

New teachers need a strong mentor who has positive beliefs centering on teacher development. The mentor must believe that teachers can successfully enter the field via various routes. If the mentor is philosophically opposed to teachers from alternative programs, then a different mentor needs to be selected by the principal. The mentor can provide specific types of support that can help retain the alternative program candidate.

The Department Chair or Team Leader

The third contact for new teachers is the subject department chair or grade-level team leader. Giving the new teacher a contact person who is an experienced teacher and a close-at-hand source of support can make a continuing impact on the teacher.

A FINAL NOTE

Many of the factors that cause teachers to leave are beyond your control. However, the loss of good teachers to other professions is such a serious matter that you should do all within your power to retain the best and the brightest.

Developing the Faculty as a Cohesive Community

Thus far, this book has emphasized the development of highly qualified individuals. However, a highly qualified faculty is more than the sum of its parts. This chapter explains how to develop the faculty as a cohesive community.

REFLECT ABOUT VALUES AND PRACTICES

Insightful reflection can provide a solid foundation for cohesiveness. Three kinds of reflective discussions will be of value.

Reflect About a Cohesive Community

To begin the process, lead the faculty in deliberating about the concept of the school as a *cohesive community.* Two attributes are crucial here. First, the school is characterized by cohesiveness, a belief that the faculty is a unified faculty working together. Cohesive faculty know how to resolve conflict and how to use the multiple talents of the faculty in advancing school reform. They share materials, solve problems together, and cooperate in learning together. Professional cohesiveness is desirable as a faculty trait. On the other hand, some faculties manifest excessive personal interactions. In those schools, most faculty interactions involve discussions of sports events, faculty social affairs, and faculty gossip. As Marzano (2003) notes, a few studies suggest that excessive personal interactions are correlated with lower achievement. This chapter, therefore, focuses on professional cohesiveness, not faculty partying.

Second, the school is considered a community. Many schools report that they have found the community concept an energizing and cohesive force. In a school that emphasizes the school as a community, both students and teachers hold the following beliefs (see Battistich, Solomon, Kim, Watson, & Schaps, 1995).

- We belong here. This is our school.
- We find meaning and purpose here. Our work has an impact.
- We are known here and are valued as contributing members.
- We are responsible and hold ourselves accountable.
- We can make a difference here and can influence what the school can become.
- We work together for the common good.

Those key concepts working together can make a significant difference.

Researchers note that the community concept is especially effective in reaching and helping minority disadvantaged students (see Battistich et al., 1995).

Revisit the Work on the Highly Qualified Teacher

As part of the deliberative process, lead the faculty in revisiting the four documents that delineate the faculty conception of highly qualified teachers: the nature of quality learning, the essential skills of teaching, the subject skills, and the hallmarks of professionalism. These discussions should determine if these documents reflect the best current knowledge and the faculty's present values.

Hold Reflective Discussions on Controversial Issues

Divisiveness often occurs when teachers argue about current educational issues. For example, in the 1980s and 1990s, some faculties became sharply divided on the issue of phonics versus whole language in the teaching of reading.

Rather than reasoning objectively about the issue, they assumed partisan positions, getting angry and arguing heatedly. The principal needs to provide leadership here in creating and sustaining what Freidus (2000) calls "discourse communities." In such schools, teachers learn how to reason and reflect in a professional manner. Rather than choosing sides, teachers would reason through a process such as the following:

1. Does the school system have a policy statement on the issue that might constrain or support our efforts?

2. What aspects of whole language are supported by the research?

3. What is the quality of that research?

4. What aspects of a phonics approach are supported by the research?

5. What is the quality of that research?

6. What has been the experience of our teachers in teaching beginning reading?

7. Based on our study of the issue, what actions, if any, should we take with our reading program?

In holding such discussions, avoid letting the discussion become a blaming or complaining session.

COMMUNICATE COHESIVENESS

Communication plays a vital role in achieving cohesiveness. Three aspects seem important here.

Speak the Language of Cohesiveness

One important step is to speak the language of a cohesive community. In this sense, the principal acts as a preacher who openly advocates a cohesive community. In faculty meetings, in parent sessions, and in conferences with students, the school leaders should stress the values of cohesiveness, using such language as the following:

- We are united.
- We are a team.
- We work together.
- We are unified.
- We are a family of learners.

Develop a Common Language

The language that faculty use in talking about teaching and learning can serve as a force for cohesiveness—or complicate communication. One useful activity here is to hold a meeting to develop a common language. Divide the faculty into small heterogeneous groups, with each group composed of teachers representing different grade levels and subjects. Assign one of the essential skills to each group. The group is responsible for restating its essential skill into teacher-friendly language. When the groups have finished their task, each makes a brief presentation to the faculty. After sufficient discussion by the entire faculty, a formal statement of the common language is formulated. To illustrate the importance of this work, consider these examples.

Original Wording

Develops, uses, and shares problem-solving units based on curriculum standards

Revised Versions

Plans units based on curriculum standards

Plans with curriculum standards

Makes unit plans based on curriculum standards

Uses state standards in planning

Each restatement is different from the rest in wording and emphasis. However, the process results in the faculty feeling greater ownership of the list.

Take a Firm Stand Against Bias and Stereotyping

Unfortunately, there are still a small number of teachers who are biased against women (especially women administrators) and members of ethnic minorities. While such closed-mindedness seems less egregious these days than a few decades ago, it is still apparent in many faculties, manifesting itself in racist jokes, subtle innuendo, and stereotypical comments. The principal needs to make clear at the outset and at all appropriate times thereafter that such language and behavior will not be tolerated. And clearly, the principal needs to avoid these biases in speech and action.

REINFORCE COHESIVENESS

Cohesiveness needs to be reinforced from time to time through the actions of administrators and other leaders. Four specific actions will be crucial.

Recognize and Reward Faculty Who Demonstrate Cohesiveness

One important means of shaping the culture of the school is to recognize and reward faculty who demonstrate the desired traits. The recognition can come by simply praising teachers who have worked effectively together and promoted unity. Some faculties also have found it effective to recognize a "Unifier of the Year," a teacher who has provided outstanding service that united the faculty.

Use Cooperative Development as a Structure for Success

As noted previously, cooperative development is an effective process for developing competent, experienced teachers. It is also an effective strategy for achieving long-term school improvement. In the process, it develops cohesiveness among the team members (see Sagor, 1992).

Experience has shown that the following guidelines will facilitate success. First, use the existing team structure rather than adding another layer to faculty structure. This means that elementary and middle schools should use grade-level teams, whereas high schools should use subject departments. Encourage the teams to set challenging learning goals, even if they might require more time for their attainment. Require each team to demonstrate how its developmental goal is directly related to student learning. Wherever feasible, provide in-school released time for teams to meet and work together. Finally, recognize and reward team accomplishment.

To increase the cohesiveness, help each team share its work with the rest of the faculty. Two methods seem effective here. First, each team can write an article explaining what it accomplished and learned. Those articles can be published in a school-produced journal. The second method is to hold an action research forum, in which each team makes a presentation.

Serve as a Role Model

If the principal wants teachers to collaborate and receive feedback from peers, then the principal should serve as a role model by working with peer administrators (see Krovetz, 1993). In such programs, two or more principals agree to meet for their own development. To improve conference skills, one principal observes as another one confers with a teacher. Then the observer gives the colleague objective feedback about the conference. To improve problem-solving skills, one principal presents a problem to a group of colleagues and asks them to explain how they would solve the problem. They discuss their problem-solving approaches.

Emphasize the Importance of Deprivatized Practice

In too many schools, teachers attempt to "privatize practice." As scholars use the term, it refers to teachers' attempts to take ownership of teaching strategies, holding them close to their chests. In cohesive school faculties, teachers willingly share ideas, techniques, and materials. The principal can encourage teachers to deprivatize practice by giving teams time for group planning, devoting time at each faculty meeting for "teaching tips" discussions, and praising teachers who willingly share what they have learned (Bryk, Camburn, & Seashore, 1997; Hashimoto & Abbott, 1996).

MAKE SPECIAL EFFORTS

In addition to these general approaches, school leaders should be sensitive to the influences of special groups and special times.

Be Sensitive to the Needs of Special Groups in the School

Faculties often develop group rivalries that can become a divisive force. For example, we found that teachers teaching vocational courses in a comprehensive high school often considered themselves outsiders, in opposition to teachers teaching academic courses. The solution here was to identify "boundary spanners," who belonged to both groups. The boundary spanners were able to minimize group conflict since they were able to influence both groups (Gremillion & Cody, 1998). The boundary spanners were also able to clarify misunderstandings, since they had detailed knowledge of how each group had made decisions.

Reach Out to Faculty Isolates

Some faculty members are isolates, loners who do not feel part of any group. The principal should make special efforts to include them in all activities, even providing opportunities for leadership. These actions should be accompanied by informal counseling, to determine how the isolate feels about his or her relationships with the rest of the faculty. Some highly competent teachers do not want to get involved with committee work and special assignments. One such faculty member put it this way:

> I will teach as best as I can and carry out my nonteaching responsibilities but my family comes first. And right now my family is taking up all of my nonteaching time.

Provide Special Support at Times of High Stress

When high-stress events occur, such as the release of scores on high-stakes tests, the principal should be sure to give teachers the special support they need. At such times, local newspapers often publish headlined stories, especially if the results have been less than satisfactory. The principal can prevent sharp decreases in teacher morale by assuring the teachers that they are not solely to blame for the decline. The positive slant can be accompanied by a focus on what the school can do to improve scores in the next round of testing.

Provide Support in School Reform Efforts

There is some evidence that school reform efforts are especially taxing for teachers, often creating divisiveness (see Pechman & King, 1993). Teachers spend additional time in implementing reforms, which have often been imposed from on high. They are expected to function in new roles, such as team leaders and mentors. Those new roles require them to acquire and use new skills in highly visible contexts. This combination of factors creates stress, which can manifest itself in combativeness and withdrawal. The principal needs to understand how reform efforts can often be counterproductive by creating weighty burdens for teachers. While such supportive stances are always welcome, school leaders should also convey to teachers the excitement of meaningful reform and the joy that comes from growth.

References

Arends, R. I., & Rigazio-DiGilio, A. J. (2000). *Beginning teacher induction.* East Lansing, MI: National Center for Research on Teacher Learning. (ERIC Documentation Reproduction Service No. ED450074)

Bambino, D. (2002). Critical friends. *Educational Leadership, 59*(6), 25–27.

Battistich, V., Solomon, D., Kim, D., Watson, M., & Schaps, E. (1995). Schools as communities, poverty levels of student populations, and students' attitudes, motives, and performance: A multilevel analysis. *American Educational Research Journal, 32,* 627–658.

Bryk, A., Camburn, E., & Seashore, K. (1997). *Professional community in Chicago elementary schools.* East Lansing, MI: National Center for Research on Teacher Learning. (ERIC Document Reproduction Service No. ED412624)

Calhoun, E. F. (2002). Action research for school improvement. *Educational Leadership, 59*(6), 18–24.

California Commission on Teacher Credentialing. (1992). *Success for beginning teachers.* Sacramento, CA: Author.

Clement, M. C. (2000). *How to interview, hire, and retain high-quality new teachers.* Alexandria, VA: National Association of Elementary School Principals.

Clewell, B. C., Darke, K., Davis-George, T., Forcier, L., & Manes, S. (2000). *Literature review on teacher recruitment programs.* Washington, DC: U.S. Department of Education.

Clewell, B. C., & Villegas, A. M. (2001). *Absence unexcused: Ending teacher shortages in high-need areas.* Washington, DC: Urban Institute Press.

Collins, T. (1999). *Attracting and retaining teachers in rural areas.* Charleston, WV: ERIC Clearinghouse on Rural Education and Small Schools.

Cotton, K. (1995). *Research you can use to improve results.* Alexandria, VA: Association for Supervision and Curriculum Development.

Danielson, C. (1996). *Enhancing professional practice.* Alexandria, VA: Association for Supervision and Curriculum Development.

Danielson, C., & McGreal, T. L. (2000). *Teacher evaluation to enhance professional practice.* Alexandria, VA: Association for Supervision and Curriculum Development.

Darling-Hammond, L. (1997). *Doing what matters most: Investing in quality teaching.* Kutztown, PA: National Commission on Teaching and America's Future.

Darling-Hammond, L., & McLaughlin, M. W. (1995). Policies that support professional development in an era of reform. *Phi Delta Kappan, 76*(8), 597–604.

Flood, J., Lapp, D., Squire, J. R., & Jensen, J. M. (Eds.). (2003). *Handbook of research on teaching the English language arts* (2nd ed.). New York: Macmillan.

Fox, J. E., & Certo, J. (1999). *Recruiting and retaining teachers: A review of the literature.* Richmond, VA: Metropolitan Educational Research Consortium.

Freidus, H. (2000). *Fostering reflective practice.* East Lansing, MI: National Center for Research on Teacher Learning. (ERIC Document Reproduction Service No. ED441787)

Fullan, M. (2001). *The new meaning of educational change* (3rd ed.). New York: Teachers College Press.

Fullan, M. G. (1995). The limits and the potential of staff development. In T. R. Guskey & M. Huberman (Eds.), *Professional development in education* (pp. 253–268). New York: Teachers College Press.

Gall, M. D., & Vojtek, R. O. (1994). *Planning for effective staff development.* Eugene: University of Oregon Press.

Glatthorn, A. A. (1997). *Differentiated supervision* (2nd ed.). Alexandria, VA: Association of Supervision and Curriculum Development.

Glatthorn, A. A. (1999). *Performance standards and authentic learning.* Larchmont, NY: Eye on Education.

Glatthorn, A. A., & Fontana, J. (Eds.). (2000). *Coping with standards, tests, and accountability.* Washington, DC: National Education Association.

Glatthorn, A. A., & Sheerer, M. (2004). *The teacher's portfolio* (2nd ed.). Lancaster, PA: ProActive.

Glickman, C. D. (2002). *Leadership for learning: How to help teachers succeed.* Alexandria, VA: Association for Supervision and Curriculum Development.

Goals 2000: Educate America Act. (n.d.). 103d Third Cong. Accessed from www.ed.gov/legislation/GOALS2000/TheAct/index.htm

Green, J. E., & Smyser, S. O. (1996). *The teacher portfolio: A strategy for professional development and evaluation.* Lancaster, PA: Technomics.

Green, P. C. (1996). *Get hired! Winning strategies to ace the interview.* Austin, TX: Bard Press.

Gremillion, J., & Cody, C. (1998). *Understanding teacher relationships during a mandated reform.* East Lansing, MI: National Center for Research on Teacher Learning. (ERIC Document Reproduction Service No. ED419889)

Grouws, D. A. (Ed.). (1992). *Handbook of research on mathematics teaching and learning.* New York: Macmillan.

Guskey, T. R. (2002). Does it make a difference? Evaluating professional development. *Educational Leadership, 59*(6), 45–51.

Hargreaves, A., & Dawe, R. (1990). Paths of professional development: Contrived collegiality, collaborative culture, and the case of peer coaching. *Teaching and Teacher Education, 6,* 227–241.

Hashimoto, F. K., & Abbott, D. E. (1996). *Conflicts in school restructuring.* East Lansing, MI: National Center for Research on Teacher Learning. (ERIC Document Reproduction Service No. ED396412)

Houston, W. R., Marshall, F., & McDavid, T. (1993). Problems of traditionally prepared and alternatively certified new teachers. *Education and Urban Society, 26*(1), 78–89.

Jailall, J. (1998). *Differentiated supervision revisited.* Doctoral dissertation, East Carolina University.

Klug, B. J., & Salzman, S. A. (1990). *Formal induction vs. informal mentoring: Comparative effects and outcomes.* East Lansing, MI: National Center for Research on Teacher Learning. (ERIC Document Reproduction Services No. ED323628)

Krovetz, M. L. (1993). Collegial learning communities. *School Community Journal, 3,* 71–84.

Lawrence, C. E., Vachon, M. K., Leake, D. O., & Leake, B. H. (1993). *The marginal teacher.* Thousand Oaks, CA: Corwin.

Little, J. W. (1990). The mentor phenomenon and the social organization of teaching. In C. Cazden (Ed.), *Review of research in education 16* (pp. 297–352). Washington, DC: American Educational Research Association.

Marso, R. N., & Pigge, F. L. (1990). *Teacher mentor assessment programs.* East Lansing, MI: National Center for Research on Teacher Learning. (Education Document Service No. ED322114)

Marzano, R. J. (2003). *What works in schools.* Alexandria, VA: Association for Supervision and Curriculum Development.

Marzano, R. J., & Kendall, J. S. (1999). *Essential knowledge.* Aurora, CO: Mid-Continent Regional Educational Laboratory.

McCreight, C. (2000). *Teacher attrition, shortage, and strategies for teacher retention.* Austin: Texas A & M University.

McLaughlin, M. W., & Talbert, J. E. (1993). How the world of students and teachers challenges policy coherence. In S. H. Fuhrman (Ed.), *Designing coherent education policy.* San Francisco: Jossey-Bass.

Mertz, N. T., & McNeely, S. R. (2001, April). *Blind man's bluff: Instructional leadership, teacher selection, and rational decision making.* Paper presented at the annual meeting of the American Educational Research Association, Seattle, WA.

Moir, E. (1999). The stages of a teacher's first year. In M. Scherer (Ed.), *A better beginning* (pp. 19–26). Alexandria, VA: Association for Supervision and Curriculum Development.

Murphy, C. U., & Lick, D. (2001). *Whole faculty study groups* (2nd ed.). Thousand Oaks, CA: Corwin.

National Center for Education Statistics. (2001). *Teacher preparation and professional development: 2000.* Washington, DC: U.S. Department of Education, Office of Educational Research and Improvement.

National Commission on Teaching and America's Future. (1996). *What matters most: Teaching for America's future.* Woodbridge, VA: Author.

National Research Council. (1999). *Improving student learning.* Washington, DC: Author.

National Staff Development Council. (2001). *Standards for staff development.* Oxford, OH: Author.

Natriello, G., & Zumwalt, K. (1992). Challenges to an alternative route for teacher education. In A. Lieberman (Ed.), *The changing contexts of teaching* (pp. 59–78). Chicago: University of Chicago Press.

Pechman, E. M., & King, J. A. (1993). *Obstacles to restructuring.* New York: NCREST Teachers College, Columbia University.

Podsen, I. J., & Denmark, V. M. (2000). *Coaching and mentoring first year and student teachers.* Larchmont, NY: Eye on Education.

Robinson, G. W. (1998). *New teacher induction: A study of selected new teacher induction models and common practices.* East Lansing, MI: National Center for Research on Teacher Learning. (ERIC Document Reproduction Services No. ED424219)

Rohrbeck, C. A., Ginsburg-Block, M. D., Fantuzzo, J. W., & Miller, T. R. (2003). Peer-assisted learning interventions with elementary school students: A meta-analytic review. *Journal of Educational Psychology, 95,* 258–267.

Routman, R. (2002). Teacher talk. *Educational Leadership, 59*(6), 32–35.

Sagor, R. I. (1992). *Collaborative action research.* East Lansing, MI: National Center for Research on Teacher Learning. (ERIC Document Reproduction Service No. ED350705)

Shulman, L. S. (1986, February). Those who understand: Knowledge growth in children. *Educational Researcher, 15*(2), 4–14.

Shulman, L. S. (1987). Knowledge and teaching: Foundations of the new reform. *Harvard Educational Review, 57,* 1–22.

Simmons, A. (2000). *Guide to today's teacher recruitment challenges.* Belmont, MA: Recruiting New Teachers.

Southeast Center for Teaching Quality. (2001). *Recruitment and retention strategies in a regional and national context.* Chapel Hill, NC: Author.

Sparks, D. (1995). Focusing staff development on improving student achievement. In G. Cawelti (Ed.), *Handbook of research on improving student achievement* (pp. 163–169). Arlington, VA: Educational Research Service.

Sparks, D., & Hirsh, S. (1997). *A new vision for staff development.* Alexandria, VA: Association for Supervision and Curriculum Development.

Stiggins, R. J., & Duke, D. L. (1988). *The case for commitment to teacher growth: Research on teacher evaluation.* Albany: State University of New York Press.

Sweeny, B. W. (2001). *Leading the teacher induction and mentoring program, K–college.* Arlington Heights, IL: SkyLight Professional Development.

U.S. Department of Education. (1998). *Promising practices: New ways to improve teacher quality.* Washington, DC: Author.

Watanabe, T. (2002). Learning from Japanese lesson study. *Educational Leadership, 59*(6), 36–39.

Weiss, E. M., & Weiss, S. G. (1999). *Beginning teacher induction: ERIC digest.* Washington, DC: ERIC Clearinghouse on Teaching and Teacher Education.

Williams, B. (1993). Skill fixation in staff development. *Educational Technology Journal, 4*(20), 1993.

Zemelman, S., Daniels, H., & Hyde, A. (1998). *Best practice* (2nd ed.). Portsmouth, NH: Heinemann.

Index

NSDC's mission is to ensure success for all students by serving as the international network for those who improve schools and by advancing individual and organization development.

CORWIN PRESS

The Corwin Press logo—a raven striding across an open book—represents the union of courage and learning. Corwin Press is committed to improving education for all learners by publishing books and other professional development resources for those serving the field of PreK–12 education. By providing practical, hands-on materials, Corwin Press continues to carry out the promise of its motto: **"Helping Educators Do Their Work Better."**